AUDACIOUS LEADERSHIP

How to become a leader that is bold,
innovative, inventive and unconstrained
by previous ideas.

This book is dedicated to my wife, Debbie.

Without your consistent encouragement, patience, dedication and thought provoking questions this book would never have become a reality.

CONTENTS

To find out more about me or to access

my videos, podcasts, audio series, free downloads

and courses, please visit my website www.vicwilliams.net

Also connect with me on LinkedIn
www.linkedin.com/in/vicwilliams1

or

follow me on Twitter https://twitter.com/AudaciousCo

ACKNOWLEDGEMENTS

This book grew out of a desire to understand leadership which began developing at a relatively young age. From my earliest recollection, I have derived enormous pleasure from reading about historical events and developed a particular passion for both World Wars. It was this passion which has driven my desire to understand leaders and leadership. From political leaders such as Abraham Lincoln, Winston Churchill, Margaret Thatcher and Nelson Mandela to business leaders such as Thomas Edison, Leonardo Da Vinci, Marie Curie, Warren Buffett, Bill Gates and Henry Ford, and so many more, I have asked questions about their individual characteristics, behaviours & traits.

I have looked at their family background, as well as their financial, social, educational and political status and asked whether they were born to lead or if some force compelled them to lead and others to follow. I have tried to discover whether there was a specific event which caused them to be recognised as a leader or did they develop into a leader over time.

Due to or in spite of this passion to understand leadership, I have, throughout my life, often either found myself in leadership roles or observing people in leadership roles and asking questions about how I or they stack up to the leaders I have studied. From managing a restaurant and owning a busy automotive workshop to CEO of a multi-million-pound financial practice and facilitating a multi practice merger, I have experience many leadership challenges. On some occasions I have failed and have learnt what does not work in those circumstances, but on most occasions I have been able to apply the lessons I have learned successfully.

I have been married to Debbie for over 20 years during which time she has seen me at my best and at my worst. In all of this time, whether during good times or bad, Debbie has never given me anything other than the most incredible, unreserved support and encouragement. Never once in the years of our marriage has she ever had a negative word to say about me or to me. Whether in public or in private, Debbie is always the same. It completely astonishes me every day and I know that without her, this book nor any other venture I enter into would exist. I have been able to talk with her as a friend and advisor as well as a wife for all these years, which has daily added value to our lives. I am truly a blessed man.

There are also so many other people who have been examples of great leadership and have encouraged me in all I have done throughout my life. Too many to mention in the short space of this book and without wanting to cause offence to any whom I don't mention, I do want to acknowledge, Arnold, Valme, Ingrid, Aran, Justin, Brett and Darren. Each of you have challenged my thinking and perspective on leadership. For this I thank you.

INTRODUCTION

"The rarest commodity on earth is not food, water, gold or diamonds. We have the capacity to resolve or find all of these. The rarest commodity is wise leadership without ego".

Author unknown.

Despite hundreds of years of study around the topic of leadership and its implications on people, nations, governments and business, there is as yet no clear and definitive conclusion which has universally been bought into. Over the past two hundred years or so many theories and ideas have emerged about leadership and the types of people who become leaders.

Many of these thoughts and ideas stand in direct contradiction to each other, and while many have been rejected or discredited to some degree and others are too strictly defined to take into account human individuality, personalities and unique perspectives, there remain large swaths of people who still hang onto and attempt to adhere to them.

The fact is that most of these ideas, thoughts and theories have largely remained focused in the 'what' of leadership rather than the 'how' and 'why'. Although more contemporary ideas, thoughts and research on leadership seem to have had a deeper scientific methodology supporting them while being flexible enough to account for individuals, they too, remain focused on the 'what' rather than 'how to' or 'why'. Many authors focus on finding the answers to questions that have long been asked and not answered, instead of changing the question altogether.

I would argue that the questions around leadership need to make a fundamental shift from 'what' type of questions to 'how to' and 'why' type of question, starting with the why of leadership.

While I am not a University or college professor, I have written this book based on personal experiences gained from leadership positions as well as from working with business, social, religious and community leaders in South Africa and the United Kingdom. My research, which is based on interviews with leaders in varying environments and across a wide range of sectors, has shown two consistent themes regarding the requirements and challenges leaders face today, and in the future.

These two themes are the increasing complexity of the business environment and the fast changing technological and generational differentials.

As the world daily becomes more and more connected and instant, leaders will require greater flexibility, be more adaptable and mobile. Since the 2007/2008 economic crash and the subsequent recession, society, industries, technologies and work environments, have continually and rapidly changed, with some environments almost unrecognisable from 5 or 10 years ago.

By way of illustration of this rapid change, 2012 saw the number of smart phones worldwide reach 1 billion. Having taken 14 years to reach this level, by the end of 2016 that number will be 2 billion worldwide and this number will continue to escalate as we become more mobile reliant.

This rapid growth in smart technology has changed the communication dynamic in business providing leaders with a set of challenges earlier generations would not have had to confront and deal with. Access to instant messaging, for example, has allowed good, and in particular bad news to travel at speeds and ways that 20 years ago we could not have predicted. Bad news has often travelled around the world before many locals even know what has happened.

For example, social media responded immediately to the Paris terror attacks on the 13th November 2015 and to the March 22nd 2016 attacks in Brussels, while the local and international media were still looking for information regarding these events. Most of the world heard of these events first via social media, in some cases while the events were unfolding.

Business decisions and responses are expected to be faster, collaborations have become farther reaching, traditional access to decision makers has been removed and there is the challenge of separating business from personal life. None of these were issues for political, business or social leaders in the past. Prior to the early 2000's, corporate boards could take time to think through challenges, make decisions and know their responses would take at least a few hours to get around. Today that has changed to the speed of a tweet or a Facebook message, the message is out and often incorrect.

Generational changes have also become more rapid and the responses of different generations to leadership has itself become a leadership challenge. Each of the definable generations brings with it a unique set of qualities and insights which, while providing diversity in the workplace, can and often do produce a stressful and demanding environment for leaders from previous generations.

For example, Generation Y, who have never known a world without mobile technology, the internet, social media or apps, are highly aspirational and are at the forefront of the push to work faster, more efficiently and in a less structured formal fashion. This is forcing business and organisational leaders to view transparency, knowledge transfer, organisational structures and internal cultural awareness from a continually changing perspective.

We have also seen a massive change in society and social norms, which continue to provide additional challenges to leaders today. Research by the US Census Bureau has shown that the average American will hold 7 to 8 different jobs before the age of 30. I recall my grandfather's pride when he received a gold watch from the gold mine he had worked at for 40 years. How the world has changed!

This complexity in the business environment and changing generational dynamic, has highlighted the need for less of the 'what' type of training and coaching of leaders and more of the 'how' and 'why' type of training and coaching.

In writing this book, I have used a number of stories, both personal and experiential for clarification or illustrative purposes and have in some cases changed the names of people concerned for privacy sake. I have also on occasions left out company and place names for the same reasons. I have attempted to make this book as practical and informative as possible using my knowledge, research and perspectives.

Finally, it needs to be said that although I use Abraham Lincoln, Winston Churchill and Nelson Mandela as examples of great leaders, I am by no means suggesting that I or any person reading this book needs to reach similar heights of fame and recognition to be a great leader. The character and qualities of these men have been widely written about and history tells their stories over and over again.

The fact is most of us will have an impact on a relatively small group of people compared to these 3 men and we may not enter the annuals of history or even reach the heights of fame some leaders do. We are more likely be the small 'l' in leadership rather than the big 'L', but that should not mean we must not strive to be the absolute best leaders we can be and have the impact we can have. We never know whose life we may influence and what they could potentially accomplish.

We should also take note that in the business world, organisational success is very closely connected to the quality and courage of its leadership.

CHAPTER 1

Leadership:
The Search.
The Why!

"Leadership is not a noun. It is a verb."

John Maxwell

LEADING
YOURSELF

DEVELOPING
NEW LEADERS

LEADING
YOUR TEAM

LEADING
ORGANISATIONS

LEADING
LEADERS

It was a humid, very dark, scary night and the mostly African crowd, armed with knobkerries, panga's and rocks was angry. Murderously and vengefully angry. And that anger was being vented on a small, lightly armed and utterly terrified group of young, white conscript soldiers in the middle of a township just outside the South African city of Port Elizabeth. Earlier in the day a bomb had exploded at the local community Council offices, killing 1 person and injuring 5 others. It was January 1983 and South African townships were not safe places for anyone, let alone young white soldiers. These 4 young men, not yet in their 20's, had become separated from their larger formation an hour earlier. Their unit had been sent to the township to assist the police in restoring order after the bombing, but had only served to inflame the situation further.

The crowd grew in number and in a desire for some kind of retribution and right in front of them were the potential victims of that desire. There was little the 4 men could do, given they had very limited ammunition, no experience in the situations or room to manoeuvre. They knew they were in real trouble when a group of residence began burning petrol doused tyres in a circle around them.

It was then, that a young African man not much older than the solders, but who seemed to be respected by the crowd stepped forward and began to berate the group for their actions. His words seemed to calm them down and as he reasoned with them, many began to disperse. After a while, he turned to the 4 men and told them they could go, even gave them directions to find their unit. He was a man of obvious courage and was recognised, despite his relative youth, by the crowd as a leader. They accepted his word and his command, never challenging him in any way.

Where do such people come from? Are they born or do they over time develop leadership skills? We need more leaders who, despite the situation or the odds, are willing to stand up and lead.

The question of what leadership is, how it's done, who is a leader, etc, has been and still is one of the most researched and discussed topics for philosophers, political strategist, business analysts, theorists, professors, authors and trainers. Thousands of books and article have been written, training programs designed and speeches given on the subject. Corporations, large and small, have been built on this research and every day thousands of people around the world are trained in one theory of leadership or another.

And yet it remains one of the least understood concepts across all cultures and throughout various civilizations.

In the earliest days of this research and the discussions it developed, it was believed that all leaders were born. It was postulated by Greek philosophers and later by scholars and researchers that leadership was the preserve of the few who were born at a certain level and into certain family lines which gave the responsibility of leadership to that individual.

The Greek philosopher and mathematician Plato, for example, believed only a very special, select few individuals who had superior wisdom, intellect and birth rite could become leaders. He, of course, counted himself in that select few, which made him, by his definition a leader! And it was Aristotle who suggested, *"From the moment of birth, some are marked for subjugation and others for command."* He, of course, believed he was born for command. With these philosophies, the idea that leaders are born found a beginning.

This further developed the notion of leaders being chosen by a supreme being, force or God through birth and was promoted by bishops, popes, kings, queens, princes and those within the aristocratic realm, who had an obvious vested interest promoting the idea! The fact that this was heavily supported and promoted by the Catholic and other major churches in a European context as well as by the other major religious organisations in other parts of the world, made it the prevalent leadership influence worldwide from as far back as I can find information. This thought also gave rise to concepts such as the Divine Right of Kings, along with all the abuses of people, kingdoms, countries and cultures that followed that philosophy.

Through the writing and lectures of people such as Scottish philosopher Thomas Carlyle and American scholar Fredrick Adam Woods, the theory of the 'Great Man' or 'hero' was developed, suggesting that at various times in history heroes like Shakespeare, Luther and Napoleon would rise and lead. Carlyle set out in his book, 'On Heroes, Hero-Worship and the Heroic in History,' how he saw history having turned on the decisions of heroes, describing the influence over events of such men.

Woods investigated leaders from the early 12th century through to the French Revolution and the influence they had on events of their time. From this research he concluded *'The conditions of each reign were found to approximate the ruler's capabilities.'* He further wrote, *'the man makes the nation and shapes it in accordance to his abilities.'* The hero would shape the nation, its people, business and its future.

Although this idea was mostly dropped during World War 2 as very few people wanted to see Hitler and his henchmen in a heroic light, some researches and scholars still hold to this theory today. They point to faltering businesses which are turned around by transformational leaders with 'hero' like status such as Steve Jobs (Apple), Dan Hesse (Sprint), Alan Mulally (Ford) and Harriet Green (Thomas Cook) as proof of the 'Great Man' theory in contemporary action and business.

Sir Francis Galton (1822 – 1911) took the concept of the great man a step further in his book, 'Hereditary Genius' by suggesting great leaders possessed traits that were immutable and could not be developed in others. These traits, he suggested, were unique to these extra-ordinary people, of which oddly enough he was one, and would cause them to excel in their leadership role. These would include high levels of intelligence, a sense of responsibility, creativity and a persuasive oratorical ability. From this work and the research of other scholars, a theory arose which eventually became known as trait theory and was prevalent through the 1930's and 40's.

Despite many studies analysing traits of leaders across the ages designed to establish the reliability of trait theory, the only common and consistent trait that has been found to reliably exist is the average leader is slightly taller and slightly more intelligent and as a result trait theory has fallen way short of an accurate predictor of great leadership or in fact of any form of leadership!

Where trait theory focused on leaders being born with characteristics that made them leaders, behaviour theory suggested certain behaviours were instead responsible for the leadership abilities of individuals. This brought about the rise of psychometric testing in the 1950's with the work of Robert McHenry and with it new leadership models, which attempted to identify those behaviours inherent in individuals who would become great leaders. Companies around the world have spent, and still do spend, millions of pounds, dollars, yen or Euro's on psychometric testing in the hopes of finding the individual with great leadership potential.

I have personally done many psychometric tests over the years for a variety of roles and as a part of my research on leadership, mostly with widely differing results. I have also used a wide selection of the tests available in working with different clients and have seen some great results and some really odd results. From DISC and Myers-Briggs Typology Indicator to FIRO-B and VIA Inventory of Strength, most have value in guiding you to understand leadership potential in people, but all have differing perspectives, so will give very different results. This is a word of caution!

Since trait theory, we have had contingency theory, transactional theory, transformational theory, power & influence theory, emotionally intelligent leaders, along with a host of other ideas, theories and a few wild and woolly suggestions.

Contingent theory, for example, argues there is no single way of leading and every leader should make decisions based on the situations with which they are confronted. This suggests that leaders are only leaders in situations which suit their skill set and would in that particular environment perform at a high level. Transactional theory is characterised by a transaction between the leader and the follower, while power & influence theory relies on the different ways a leader will use power and/or influence in order to deliver whatever they need to get done.

Emotional intelligence in leadership suggests that E.I. is twice as important as technical skills therefore the leader who is best able to manage their behaviour and interpersonal skills would be a great leader. With so much discussion on the subject of emotional intelligence, I'm never sure whether it's a theory, a type or a style of leadership.

Apart from these theories, we have a whole host of types and styles of leadership, all with a myriad of detractors, adherent's, supporters, scholars and research backing their individual validity. From servant leadership and authentic leadership to chaos and strategic leadership, there is no widely accepted definition of leadership, leaders or leading. Most of these theories, ideas and thoughts about leadership are in general backward looking and are seemingly focused on a world that was, not which is and toward which we are inexorably and constantly moving.

While this book is not about defining or redefining leadership or about arguing the merits of the various theories and ideas, it is about the search for leadership, understanding how to become a leader and recognising that the search for the 'why' of leadership goes on. With this in mind, it is becoming more apparent that in order to understand leadership and to develop great leaders, we should not focus solely on the individual, but on the followers and the impact the individual leader has on other individuals, teams, organisations, other leaders within the organisation and on developing new leaders.

Leadership must be seen against this backdrop and, I believe, leadership will be seen and understood as more collaborative, where partnerships are formed across the organisation to bring the collective capacity and ideas of individuals at various levels into the room and to the table. Over the past 25 plus years of working for and with a variety of leaders, with differing cultural backgrounds, education levels, family histories and generational differences, I have yet to find any one leadership theory, concept or idea that fits an individual snugly or is uniformly true.

It is also obvious to me when considering all the theories, that leadership does not belong exclusively to one individual or one group within an organisation. Leaders arise at a multitude of levels, in various roles and in a variety of circumstances. Experience and research shows an individual may lead in one area and be a follower in another within the same business or organisation. These theories also show clearly that there is no one-size-fits-all to leadership, except that intentionality and influence play dominant roles.

I have often been asked the question, *'Why do we need great leaders today?'* I think the answer to what could be a complex question is fairly simple. Great leaders make for great organisations, whether these are for-profit or not-for-profit organisations, political or social organisations. And great organisations benefit everyone. Great companies create great jobs, great political parties make great policy decisions and beneficial changes. Great social and not-for-profit organisations support people facing challenging and difficult situations. Great leaders without a doubt benefit everyone.

Further, it is important to understand that each of us are totally individual with completely unique, multi-dimensional and totally unpredictable characteristics. Just like everything in the known universe, humans are complex and non-linear creations, with unique perspectives, random and often chaotic thoughts, independent attitudes and voluntary reactions. It is impossible to accurately predict what any individual will do or how they will react in any given situation.

Generalisations, which most theories and ideas in the leadership space are, do not account for the individual. Humans are human, not machines. Machines can be design and built to work, unaided in a certain and predictable manner, over a period of time and as long as the machine is serviced regularly, it will do what it was designed to do for as long as it was designed to do that for. Machines do not have emotions, thoughts or fears. They do not experience love or hate, nor do they misunderstand or take people for granted.

Humans are not designed in the same way. Humans are random, emotional, thinking, fearing, elated, loving, hating and misunderstanding, fallible creatures.

However, the fact is, we have always needed great leaders, even more so since the massive transformations to the world of business since the economic disaster of the 2007/2008, the need for effective, and more importantly, great leadership has become stronger than ever before. Many research organisations, business groups and governments have argued that great leadership holds the key to unlocking the successes not only of individuals and companies across the globe, but also of regions and nations.

In an article published by McKinsey & Company titled "Why leadership-development programs fail" in January 2014, the authors raised a number of reason why effective leaders are in short supply and why we need to have effective leaders today. The research showed, when over 500 executives were asked to rank their top 3 human capital priorities both now and in the future, leadership development was included in both categories. Two thirds of respondents identified it as their number one concern. The article further showed only 7 percent of senior managers in the UK believe companies develop globally effective leaders.

My own research, albeit of a smaller sample than the McKinsey report, has shown executives in companies across the UK and other parts of the world are struggling to find leaders who have the skills and habits required to make them effective in the demanding and continually changing economic and political environment. This research has shown that only by placing leadership development on the same priority scale as organisational development and operational needs will organisations survive and thrive today and into the future.

In a 21st Century organisational environment, whether in business, not-for-profit or any other organisation type, where we see more and more global interaction, mainly through digital enablement with increasing speeds of information moving from sender to receiver, which has a growing degree of transparency and where everything big generally happens within a complex matrix, reliance on the traditional, theory based leadership development model, will simply no longer work. This focus on what was designed for yesterday has led to the most common problem in business, politics, not-for-profits, etc, today which is a lack of effective leadership, not a lack of effective management. Although we need both in every organisation, good managers are easier to find and appoint than great leaders, which makes the need to find and develop good leaders all the more important.

In this context, it is important to understand the vast gulf between leadership and management, although the two roles and functions may be performed by the same person. While there are commonalities between the two, they have very different skill sets and requirements. Both leadership and management are about developing value in people within organisations, which delivers value for and through the organisation. However, this is where the commonalities end.

Management is defined by role, position and job title, while leadership is not. Managers are most often appointed due to years of seniority, education levels, specific professional qualifications, etc and by definition have subordinates. I have noticed it is easy to be promoted or appointed to the position of a manager, put the title on your door or business card and to demand compliance, while those who call themselves leaders or have to tell you they are, usually are not. Often when I hear an individual, usually a person in a high managerial role within an organisation, calling themselves a leader I begin to look very closely at the skills and most of the time discover that they are what their title says they are, managers not leaders.

Leadership is not an appointment nor a promotion. Leaders don't put the title 'leader' on their office door, business card or hang it on a plague in their office. Rather, 'leader' is what the individual becomes.

Field Marshal William Slim's description of the difference between leadership and management is one of the best and clearest I have come across.

> *'Leadership is of the spirit compounded of*
> *personality and vision; its practice is an art.*
> *Management is of the mind, more a matter of*
> *accurate calculation, of statistics, of methods,*
> *time tables, and routine; its practice is a science.*
> *Managers are necessary;*
> *leaders are essential.'*

Most managers don't have leadership skills in their toolbox and often we find that leaders don't have management skills in theirs. I have worked with many great junior and senior managers within organisations of all sizes, in a host of different business environments, who could never be called leaders. From factory managers in meat processing plants and financial managers in large production facilities to production managers in small engineering firms in rural towns and practice managers in local surgeries. They do an excellent job for the organisation and deliver the company strategy on time and within budget, which is what they are there to do, but simply don't have the desire, the skill or the ability to see over the horizon at what is coming down the track.

Author and leadership pioneer Warren Bennis said when describing the difference between leadership and management, *"Leaders are people who do the right thing; managers are people who do things right."* A similar description was used by the late pre-eminent management consultant, Peter Drucker.

Like great management, great leadership is critical to the success of any organisation. And despite thousands of books, articles, blog posts and talks on the subject, the reality is training, coaching and mentoring by leaders to develop other leaders is of low priority to most organisation, with lip service often paid to the idea.

Which is really strange given the demands and expectations on business, political and social leaders. These demands and expectations are growing at an exponential rate and have never been higher. Leaders are expected to envisage a future for the organisation which is better than the present, guide development strategies that win, while creating and motivating a team to executing those strategies excellently. They are expected to constantly increase shareholder or public value, increase social participation, develop employee or public interaction, all while satisfying those who wish them to succeed and those who wish them to fail.

The reason for this lack of leadership development is twofold.

- Firstly, it has to do with the random inter changeable use of the terms which completely obscures the reality;

- Secondly, most organisations are run by managers, who see funding leadership development as an expense they can avoid.

It is time for the leaders in business, social enterprises, charities, politics, etc to stand up and change the culture within their organisations regarding leaders and leadership development.

What do great leaders do?

Having now understood the state of leadership research and having set out a case regarding the need for great leaders, the question becomes, *"What do great leaders do and how can I become one?"*

Becoming a great leader begins with what all great leaders know and understand. Leadership is a skill. An art. Not the right of birth. It has very little, if anything, to do with race, education, wealth, social standing, geographical location, position, rank or title. Promotion to a leadership role will define a manager not a leader. A leader defines the role; the reverse is not true. They have a vision of a future that is different from the reality of the present. The fact is that nothing is ever innovated, created, designed, done, without it first being done in the mind of someone. This is vision and when it is accompanied by action it becomes a reality.

Great leaders understand the environment in which the organisation operates and they use this understanding and interpretation of the environment to form a clear view of where the business or organisation should be going as well as the potential obstacles that may be coming down the road. They see the opportunities and the threats before most others and are able to mitigate the effects of these threats and take advantage of the opportunities that arise every day. This does not make them perfect in any way. Most great leaders are open to the opinions of others and often expect them to provide the insight they need.

Great leaders work both collectively and collaboratively with those around them and with those they draw in to ensure the success of the business, organisation, task, project, etc. While accepting individual responsibility and accountability, great leaders delegate well and create a culture of collective responsibility and accountability. This has nothing to do with blame shifting, which is often the preserve of command and control type cultures and has everything to with building trust, facilitating success and developing a habit within the organisation of continual improvement. By creating the culture of collective responsibility, great leaders foster collaboration within the various individuals and entities of the organisation.

Audacious Leaders refuse to be constrained by previous ideas or failures. They have a clear understanding that failure is an event not a person. I have often found that this type of leader is the type of person who succeeds when all indications are that failure is the only option.

In researching and writing this section of this book, I was reminded of 2 remarkable leadership efforts which I believe show Audacious Leadership at its best.

April 11th 1970, Apollo 13 was successfully launched from the Kennedy Space Centre with the intention of landing two of the crew on the moon. This was the 7th manned mission into space as a part of the Apollo space program, the 3rd mission intending to land men on the moon and, due to the regularity with which

NASA was sending rockets into space, was hardly news worthy. Most American's had lost interest in the Apollo missions and the TV networks would not broadcast live transmissions.

However, as most people know, three days into the mission things went horribly wrong in the most unpredictable manner possible. And yet it was in this unpredictable and totally unforeseen environment that some extra-ordinary leadership was shown.

56 hours into the mission and 205 000 miles from earth, while executing a routine service procedure, the crew heard a loud bang accompanied by fluctuations in electrical power and a temporary loss of communications with earth. Due to the subsequent loss of oxygen and fuel within the command module, the crew of 3 had to move into the attached lunar module in order to survive. This attached craft was designed to sustain a crew of 2 for a limited period of time. It is interesting to note, that although this had never occurred before nor was it thought to be a likely event, this move had been discussed and worked out during a training exercise at some stage prior to launch. Had it not been for this move and the preparation during training, the crew may not have returned to earth!

The crew on the ground as well as the crew in space faced two major hurdles. First and most importantly, they had to devise and execute a plan of getting the damaged space craft successfully back to earth which required highly complex mathematics and precise timing and secondly they had to work out a plan how to remove the carbon dioxide from the craft and prolong the oxygen the crew had. Two serious challenges which called for leadership at a multitude of levels within NASA, as well as innovative thinking, inventive design and a desire to succeed in spite of those who said it could not be done.

Both James Lowell, flight commander and flight director Gene Kranz knew their decisions could cost the lives of the 3 astronauts. However, all leadership decisions are inherently filled with risk to varying degrees. Leadership is not about being perfect or about winning ever battle. It is about accepting the inherent risks, standing by your decisions and involving your entire team in every aspect of the process.

Amongst many other challenges in the safe return of the crew was the problem of completely powering up the evacuated Command Module, after it had been completely shut-down, which was never designed for this kind of cold start-up. Completely new procedures, which under normal circumstances would take months, and in some cases years, to develop had to be drafted, written and tested in simulators before they were passed on to the crew. And if that were not enough, the crew had to make incredibly precise course corrections using engines which were never designed to be used in this way or for this purpose.

The calculations and adjustments made by the crew were made despite a lack of sleep, proper food and in an environment so cold condensation began to form on the inside walls of the craft. The result of this dedication and great leadership was a successful return of the crew to their families and friends.

Apollo 13, considered a successful failure, has many lessons of great leadership coursing through it. Immediately after the explosion on board the decision was taken to refocus on the priority of the mission from landing on the moon to the safe return of the crew. This may seem to be an obvious decision to make, but in making the decision, the leaders had set a course around which a strategy could be built. Secondly, the senior leadership at NASA trusted the flight directors and the crew sufficiently that they gave them not just the responsibility, but the authority to accomplish the mission.

Everyone concerned showed the value of their training and acted in a calm and professional manner and they clearly understood that every problem, no matter how extreme, had a solution.

I noted 5 great leadership qualities as I studied the events around Apollo 13. These 5 qualities are:

- **Decisions**. Tough decisions often need to be made in challenging circumstance where minimal information exists and the consequences are huge. Great leaders are willing to make those decisions and stand by the consequences.

- **Vision**. Great leaders set a big picture vision and challenge the team to achieve it, generally without giving the details of how to get it done.

- **Delegation**. Great leaders delegate well.

- **Calm professionalism**. Great leaders provide a calm and professional focus, while allowing others to do their jobs.

- **Solution**. Great leaders are solution finders not excuse makers.

The second of these events is the Chilean Mining Rescue. On the 5th August 2010 the world became aware of 33 miners trapped in the tunnels of a San Jose copper and gold mine in Chile's remote and inhospitable Atacama Desert. The mine, known for its substandard safety record, antiquated systems and some of the hardest rock formations on the planet, was also geologically unstable, with a notorious safety history. Despite the dangers of working in this and other mines in the area, men went underground every day in order to support their families, albeit for fairly meagre wages.

Trapped 700 meters below ground, the 33 miners survived for a record 69 days on limited food and water, with poor oxygen quality and very little to do. And during this period, 2 men from different ends of the social, political and economic spectrum emerged as leaders who kept men and the machines going until the miners were rescued and safe, in this time sensitive and very, very dangerous operation.

These ordinary men were required to make decisions based on the best guesses of engineers and miners from different organisations, areas of expertise and countries, all of whom had never experienced these circumstances before. The risks and effects of options available were often difficult to ascertain as were the counter-measures. They had to deal with the emotions of family members, the pressure of approximately 1 billion viewers worldwide and of a government who demanded results.

If these issues did not provide enough of a challenge, for the first 17 days, no one knew the exact location of the miners or whether they were even alive.

Chilean Mining Minister, Laurence Golborne, who conducted the rescue operation from the ground level and Crew Foreman, Luis Urzua, who led the group underground during those harrowing days, rose to the challenges they individually faced and drew others into their vision of what the rescue attempt could result in and the consequences of not trying everything possible and everything thought impossible.

Golborne who, despite having no mining experience, had been asked by the newly elected President to become the mining minister just 5 months' previously. Prior to his appointment, Golborne had served as CEO of Cencosud SA, the third largest listed retailer in Latin America, employing over 120 000 staff. Under his leadership the company had expanded into the Colombian, Peruvian and Brazilian markets. Although obviously a man familiar in a leadership role, the circumstances of the 5th August 2010 were clearly way beyond his experience. Using his expertise in business and his ability to negotiate, he very quickly took charge and enlisted the help of governments and private companies in South Africa, the United States and Chile. Although he was a constant presence at the mine, making decisions, meeting with families and briefing the media, he did not micromanage the team he had in place as he trusted their abilities and competence to achieve what he had laid out as the goal.

He took responsibility for resolving the crisis despite the government not owning the mine to ensure its success and the safe return of the trapped men. Within a very short period after arriving on the scene, Golborne had gained a full understanding of the situation as it stood at the time and knew that he would need to confront all of the issues the circumstances posed. He knew he would need to encourage, cajoled and if necessary twist arms, in order to accomplish the mission. He also knew he would have to answer to the President, the families, world media and the nation for both success and failure.

Having been empowered by President Pinera with the words "find the miners at any cost," Golborne brought all of his experience running a highly complex business to bear and using his leadership skills, created a team of some of the best analytical and engineering minds available.

While Golborne, was leading the rescue on the surface, crew foreman, Luis Urzua galvanised, organised and led the men underground. Very shortly after he realised they were trapped, Urzua insisted they remain focused on achieving the goal of being rescued. He told them he would be the last miner to be taken out of the mine. He set small tasks for each man daily which took their focus away from their predicament and kept them occupied.

In the group were men with a variety of skills and Urzua used these skills in planning various tasks. Urzua was a topographer, there were electricians, drillers, drivers, mechanics and machine operators. One of the men was also a medical worker, who was able to manage the health of the men, while other men were able to use their skills to drill for water and monitor environmental conditions. They also used their skills with the equipment to make noises which were eventually heard, giving the surface team the hope of rescuing them.

It was the leadership skills of both Golborne and Urzua which eventually led to the rescue of all 33 miners in a story which gripped millions of people around the world and has become one of the most dramatic rescues ever. These men led their respective teams to accomplish a mission which was far beyond their individual expertise or experience.

From these two incredible leaders, I learnt the following 5 lessons on leadership:

1. Experience is not essential to lead. Golborne had very little, if any, mining experience, but he still led. In his favour, he did not know what could not be achieved, so in his mind anything was possible. Often people in leadership roles are held back

41

by what they believe from experience to be impossible. Their knowledge hinders their vision.

2. Leaders never micro-manage. Managers should not either, but leaders delegate and trust those they have delegated to.

3. Accept help from those who offer and are able to deliver. Many leaders become insulated and blinkered by their environment, believing their team has all the expertise to make the dream a reality. Very often, outsourcing particular parts of a project is the best solution as it is easier to find expertise in niche organisations.

4. Provide motivation. Urzua kept everyone thinking about the goal of getting out. He gave them tasks, no matter how irrelevant the task seemed at the time. He kept them motivated. He used the skills of the men with him to ensure safety, communication and health.

5. Failure was not an option. Great leaders remove the option to fail from the table, forcing themselves and those around them to think not only in a linear fashion, but expand their thinking vertically as well.

What these leaders faced, differs very little from the challenges business, social, community and religious leaders face every day. Although challenges remain challenges and the scale of the challenges may differ, the principles and processes for success and failure for a leader remain the same.

The single biggest problem we encounter with leadership as a concept and with people in leadership roles is that most have no clear view of the future and can't see over the horizon in the business, political and social landscape. They are mostly constrained by previous experiences, ideas, ideologies and methods of working, even in this now very fast changing and dynamic landscape. This is not to suggest that experience is in anyway irrelevant. The past can and must be a great teacher and must be used to understand the mistakes of others, but the past should never be used as an indicator or a predictor of the future.

However, the future is unlike the past as circumstances, environments and people have changed. Today, opportunities and threats seem to appear much faster than in previous generations due to the advances in technology and communication. And great leaders must understand the view on the other side of tomorrow. Great leaders work hard on developing the skill of future thinking.

Although the leaders described in the previous two incidences had no prior experience of the circumstance they faced to rely on, they never used this as an excuse for failure. They took bold action and refused to fail. They knew there had to be a way of creating success and took the decisions necessary. This is what all great leaders do.

One of the most outstanding qualities of a great leader is their ability to develop a vision for a task or business. However, they don't stop at having a vision, but have developed the skill of drawing other people into that vision and empowering them to find their place within it. Leaders understand that climbing a great mountain alone is an achievement, but taking others with them, showing them the route and empowering them to find better routes in the future is leadership.

It is appropriate at this point to ask the questions, *'What is a vision and how does it work?'*

A vision is a destination you are aiming at reaching and should clearly and succinctly communicate what you are working to achieve as a business, organisation or individually. It is a vivid mental image of what you, as the leader, see coming down the road and how you want your business to look like at a specific point in time in the future to successfully engage with what you have seen down the road and around the corner. A vision is what gives your business or organisation a sense of direction, purpose and will prevent you from heading off in the wrong direction and should be informed by your values as an organisation. Your vision should be designed to inform your mission, your plan, your goals and your actions and should be the driver of your unique selling point (USP).

For example, if your business makes widgets for the shoe industry, your vision could be to become the number 1 preferred provider of widgets to the shoe industry in the United Kingdom by xxxx with a xx% market share and a reputation of providing the highest quality widgets in the industry providing widgets people insist on. This vision is informed by the changes you see coming in the next x years in the industry and know your widget is flexible enough to meet that demand.

A vision statement for your organisation is a 10 - 20, word sentence which defines your vision, without the specifics. A vision statement is very different from a statement of intent and from a mission statement.

Using the above example, your vision statement could be, *'The number 1 provider of widgets to the shoe industry which people insist on'.*

Great leaders take time to develop a vision that inspires and causes people to produce extra-ordinary effort in order to make that vision a reality. While most vision statements have a long term focus and aim for the business, short term and project specific visions are equally valuable and are often more powerful as the results can be seen quicker and can be designed to provide ongoing impetus to meet the long term vision.

Audacious leaders empower people with a long term vision that fills their lives with meaning and direction. A vision that shows them how every action they take, word they speak and thought they think will become an indispensable part of the success of the vision. They evaluate their own vision regularly in the face of changing circumstances and adjust it accordingly.

However, great leaders serve people not the vision. They do not place success before people. Any people! They clearly understand a vision is only as strong as the people who are a part of that vision, the people who are affected by the vision and the consequences of their vision. They never sacrifice people to serve the vision.

Throughout history we see men and women in leadership positions sacrifice people they regard as beneath them, on the altar of their own success. You don't have to look very far to find political and business 'leaders' who have destroyed people for their own success.

A classic example of this is the first day of the battle of the Somme in World War 1. Between the 1st July and the 18th November 1916 over 1 million men from all sides, were killed or wounded during what is considered to be the bloodiest battle in human history and included the almost 60 000 British casualties on the 1st of July alone, which is more than the total British casualties of the Crimean, Boer and Korean wars combined. This battle was the vision of a few British and French generals and their political masters who sacrificed the lives of so many young men with what was ultimately of very little if any gain. In fact, nearly 88 000 young men died for every mile the British and French forces gained.

The lives of young men sacrificed on the altar of one men's ego and ambition. A man so blinded by arrogance, previous experience and ignorance, that he refused to see or learn from the new reality of static, trench based warfare. A cavalryman by training, he failed to appreciate the technological advances which had been made over the previous few years or how to use these to his advantage. General Douglas Haig, the 'visionary' leader who conceived this horror, would later go on to be promoted to Field Marshal and to be created an Earl, even after repeating the same mistakes during what became known as the Battle of Passchendaele or the 3rd

Battle of Ypres a year later.

Great leadership requires that lessons be learned from mistakes, however, Haig never learned a single thing from either slaughter and remained a senior commander until the end of the war. Great leaders also accept the responsibility for failure, but in this case, as happens so often, subordinates were unduly blamed and dismissed from their positions.

While most often not costing physical lives, this is a daily occurrence in businesses around the world. Individuals in leadership roles who destroy people and their careers in order to ensure the vision is achieved. Statistics suggest mostly for little, if any, real definable gain!

Jack Welch, who was the CEO and chairman of General Electric from 1981 to 2001, is seen by many, particularly those students who follow his teaching and example of management, as an icon of business management and leadership success. However, questions are continually asked about the viability of his methods and their replication within other organisations, whether large or small.

During his tenure at General Electric the company's value rose by over 4000% and made over 600 acquisitions, all while the

US economy was in its longest ever economic growth phase. Unemployment was below 5% for the first time since 1973, interest rates were falling and both the NASDAQ and the Dow Jones industrial index were continually reaching new highs. From 1990 to 2000, barely a year went by without millions of new jobs being created and added to the US economy. It was not a difficult time to grow a business and make money.

The knock-on effect of this growth in the US economy was that most economies around the world grew exponentially which further fuelled the growth in the US economy. It is in this environment that Jack Welsh and the management methods he employed thrived. He was also extremely lucky in that a few days after he left General Electric, Al Qaeda attacked the United States on September 11 2001. A period of time in which everything changed, not only for GE, but for all companies and leaders around the world.

The question that remains to be asked and answered but probably never will be, is how well his leadership and management style would have survived a post 9/11 business world? Considering how Welch's hand-picked successor, Jeffrey Immelt, has had to change the way in which General Electric manages and develops its leaders and employees, I think the answer to the above question, would be 'not too well.' Welch believed that by ranking employees and firing the worst performing 10%, even if they had beaten their targets and heavily rewarding the top 20%, through a rigid and inflexible system, would build stronger and more secure teams! Known by various names, including 'rank and yank', employees were ranked 'A' 'B' and 'C' where 'C' employees were fired and 'A' employees were rewarded.

The multitude of consequences this system causes can only be hidden within an organisation the size of GE. It fosters unethical behaviour, inter-personal rivalries, office politics, 'us-versus-them' attitudes and cheating all to ensure individuals are not in that bottom 10% and therefore retain their jobs and income. It does not take individual, personal or business environmental circumstance into consideration and creates insecurity, dissatisfaction and makes people literally feel like a number. I have personally experienced this type of structure, have seen the destruction it causes to good people and the abuse it is open to when ranking or recruiting. Over and over again, this system which is accredited to Jack Welch has shown to fail clients, employees and companies as a whole. Consider Enron, Motorola in the mid 1990's, AIG around 2010 and more recently Yahoo. It also cost Ford millions in compensation payments.

John Quincy Adams said, *"If your actions inspire others to dream more, learn more, do more, and become more, you are a leader."* I can see this fitting well with the 'rank-and-yank' process, which was dropped by Immelt at GE! It is interesting to note that one of Immelt's rivals to replace Welch, Robert Nardelli, attempted to implement similar management practices at Home Depot, with disastrous consequences for the staff, clients and the shareholder, all of which had to be rescued by Frank Blake.

Research has shown that great leaders pursue excellence, not perfection and rise above mediocrity. Napoleon Bonaparte is recorded as saying that leaders are dealers in hope and they are great motivators. Keywords from both John Quincy Adams and Napoleon Bonaparte for leaders to focus on are '**inspire**', '**hope**' and '**motivate**'. I have never seen a ranking system which is designed to remove people from their positions being inspirational, providing hope or developing motivation.

I have found that great leaders have the capacity to listen and appreciate different opinions and perspectives. All the material, interviews and recordings surrounding the 2 near disasters mentioned earlier reveal that none of the leaders took any decisions in isolation and knew they could not do it on their own. We see a pattern of discussion, consultation and delegation which provides the leaders with options, different perspective and skill sets.

And great leaders develop the capacity to speak in such a manner as to cause people to want to listen. It is through this capacity and the ability to inspire, give hope and to provide a motivating environment that great leaders, develop great organisations, which in turn develop other great leaders. Great leaders do set high personal goals and have high expectations of their own performance. They consistently and persistently strive towards achieving those goals and meeting the expectations of themselves, but never at the expense of other people.

Management on the other hand is completely different. Management is about appraising capacities and abilities of people and their performances. This is not a leadership function. Leadership has never been and will never be easy. It is not to be entered into lightly. Great leaders understand that leadership is not a noun. It's a verb. It is about action. Not about standing still.

'Leaders must be close enough to relate to others, but far enough ahead to motivate them.'

John Maxwell

3 Audacious Leadership Examples

Lincoln, Churchill and Mandela.

It is appropriate at this point to consider three great leaders who span centuries, continents and ideologies and yet are widely recognised as three of the greatest leaders and examples of leadership ever. Three men who have inspired nations to see the possibilities of tomorrow as vastly different from the realities of today. Three men who inspire individuals in their generations to rise higher and become more than they may ever have become. Three men who, though often perceived as divisive, direct and even rude, were the glue that held diverse and opposing groups together to see a vision delivered. Three vary fallible, unique, non-linear, unpredictable and courageous men, who changed nations and the world of their time.

Lincoln

Abraham Lincoln was the 16th President of the United States of American and although assassinated in April 1865, he successfully led the United States through the very bitter years of the Civil War and its greatest constitutional, moral and political crisis. He is also regarded as one of the most persistent and resilient leaders of modern history as no matter the setbacks he faced, Abraham Lincoln bounced back with incredible regularity and ultimately with success. The picture we have today is one in which no failure or personal disaster could hold him back or stop him in his drive to become the American President.

Lincoln had a clear understanding of his own strengths and weaknesses. One of these weaknesses was to give some people more opportunities than they deserved, however, he was readily willing to accept blame for the failure of others and to deflect credit for success to others. Though a weakness when it comes to other people, it was a strength when it came to himself. Lincoln continuously gave himself, like he did with so many other people, another chance. He never gave up on himself.

One of his greatest strengths, however, was his ability to surround himself with men who were unafraid of challenging him and his ideas. Men who were not afraid or intimidated by him or by his position. He welcomed strong opinions which fostered thoughtful and lively debates as well as personal reflection. Lincoln was comfortable with conflict and people challenging his vision, ideas and plans. On occasions, he would accept additions or alternatives to his plans and occasionally he would drop the idea altogether as other ideas or plans were better suited.

I have noticed that all great leaders share these 2 qualities. Great leaders readily accept their weaknesses without projecting them on those around them, while welcoming debate and challenge to their ideas and plans. Weak leaders will generally allow other people to take the fall when plans fail, whether it is their fault or not.

I recently had to deal with a situation where a CEO with weak leadership abilities was too afraid to take decisive action against a director in the company and blamed all of the company's ills and misfortune on this director. This situation had persisted for about 5 years, until via the correct process and external intervention, the director was removed from his position and was dismissed from the company. The CEO then began deflecting blame for the issues on to other people, while never accepting responsibly for the process that led to the individual being appointed in the first place or for the circumstances which led to and culminated with the dismissal. This is a pattern I see repeatedly in companies I have dealings with.

Lincoln also knew the value of making decisions and the responsibility which accompanies those decisions. Great leaders understand that decisions have to be made and despite the opinions, thoughts and contributions of others, are willing to make them. Lincoln knew when he had sufficient information on which to make a decision and after spending a short time reflecting, often in solitude, would make his decision and would accept the consequences, good or bad.

Nowhere will you find any indication that all the decisions Lincoln made were the right ones nor that all of them had good outcomes. And yet, until his dying day, he continued to make decisions and stand by them, right or wrong. Great leaders are comfortable with the failure of some of their decisions and use those failures to learn and make better decisions in the future. They never allow decision failures to prevent them from making decisions that need to be made as they go forward.

As a masterful and thoughtful communicator and listener, Lincoln had the ability to make the most complex of concepts seem simple that all within his reach could understand and feel included. Being a voracious reader, he used what he had learned and absorbed to shape his grammar and eloquent speech, which resulted in the ability to communicate well. Life was a lesson to Lincoln. It caused him to appreciate others perspectives and allowed him to communicate in a manner they clearly understood.

This included communicating his aspirations, goals and beliefs in which he was uncompromising and would not waver. It was this ability to communicate well which enabled him to draw his cabinet and his nation along with him even in the darkest days when defeat seemed inevitable and there was as yet no silver lining to any cloud. The fact is, all great leaders learn to cultivate their communication in such a manner people want to listen to them, even those who stand opposed.

Communication, both listening and speaking, are key components to the success of any leader and the greater the ability the greater the leadership potential and impact.

Churchill

Churchill was the bulldog that growled and snarled when the British Empire needed strength most and when all around him, other 'leaders' were showing their weaknesses and compromised. With a strong will, direct attitude and an understanding of the needs of his people, Churchill rose to the occasion. He refused to be the dog that rolled over and played dead!

Although he understood his limitations and weaknesses more than anyone except possibly his wife, Clementine, he had a clear sense of his obligations, responsibilities and strengths. On occasions, by the force of his will, he dragged the country and the free world forward until the vision of the future became a reality. Although Churchill was very clear in his knowledge of his past successes and failures, whether real or attributed to him, he would never allow these to restrain him from heading toward the goal and prize he saw before him.

He had a vision of how the future could be so different from his present throughout his life and on most occasions took many people with him on the journey to seeing that vision become a reality. The Second World War is a perfect example of this ability, where he exhibited incredible focus and preparation for whatever was thrown at him. This allowed him to remain calm under some of the most stressful and trying circumstances imaginable.

Churchill was known for his tenacity, persistence and ability to inspire confidence in those around him, the nation at large and as well as many countries friendly to the cause. Even in the darkest days at the beginning of World War 2, he would not permit a defeatist attitude and consistently projected optimism and fortitude. Most people will recognise, even today, his famous speeches in those challenging days and his enthusiastic, encouraging visits to the most devastated parts of London, the rest of the country, as well as visiting the troops in Egypt.

The famous words he spoke in the Houses of Parliament on the 4th June 1940, *"We shall go on to the end. We shall fight in France, we shall fight on the seas and oceans, we shall fight with growing confidence and growing strength in the air, we shall defend our island, whatever the cost may be. We shall fight on beaches, we shall fight on the landing grounds, we shall fight in the fields and in the streets, we shall fight in the hills; we shall never surrender,"* showed not only this persistence, resolve and tenacity, but caused an opposition member of parliament to comment, *"That was worth 1,000 guns, and the speeches of 1,000 years."*

And this from a man who was not university educated, twice failed the entrance exam to the Royal Military College Sandhurst, had a speech impediment, suffered from depression and who took the majority of the blame for the fiasco that was the Gallipoli landing in World War 1!

Although not university educated, he was highly self-educated and as a result was not limited by conventional thinking and prescribed ideas. He was boundless in his ability to think and imagine outside of the normal, stereotypical boxes and he was obsessed with the lessons history could provide to the present and the future. He was innovative and adaptive to the circumstances and used his historical insight and imaginatively active mind to look far into the future in order to understand the consequences of decisions and actions.

Despite all these things, that he was, first and foremost a massively flawed individual who stubbornly held onto issues when most of the world had moved on. He was adept at infuriating many of his colleagues and most of his military leadership. His consumption of alcohol, food and cigars were particular vices that caused him and those around him numerous issues. He was not naturally courageous nor a man of great physical strength in spite of the image he projected.

However, his first move after being appointed Prime Minister was to form a coalition government bringing all sides into the decision making arena, while ridding the government and the senior civil service of all the advocates of appeasement. He learned the lessons from the mistakes made in the Gallipoli campaign and appointed men of substance around him. Men who were not afraid of him or afraid to challenge him. Despite his failings and the enormous pressure of the war, it is almost impossible, even with the value of hindsight, to find any other person who could have led Britain and the rest of the world through those 6 years of World War 2.

As with Lincoln, Churchill understood his strengths which he used to great effect and he understood his weaknesses, which had led to many mistakes and ill-judged decisions in the past and learned from them.

Tenacity, persistence and a will to learn and change. These are the hallmarks of a great leader. Psychiatrist and author Anthony Storr concluded, *"The more one examines Winston Churchill as a person, the more one is forced to the conclusion that his aggressiveness, his courage, and his dominance were not rooted in his inheritance, but were the product of deliberate decision and iron will."*

Although born into the aristocracy, Churchill knew he was not born a leader, but had to become a leader. He understood that it was not a right of birth and spent his life constantly recreating himself. This enabled him to recover from failures and setbacks that for many people would have been career-ending and disastrous.

Mandela

Nelson Rolihlahla Mandela is a man whose life story transcends national borders, political factions, racial boundaries, languages and cultures and the effects of his life will, with Lincoln and Churchill, live long after his death not only in the annuls of history, but also in business and leadership culture. His life, attitude, words and actions contain many valuable lessons from a man who could be considered as one of the greatest leaders in human history.

Mandela was a visionary who had the ability to see far beyond the present no matter the struggles and personal pain. For the 27 years he was imprisoned as well as the years after his release, he consistently anticipated the future and strategically positioned himself to be ready when the moment arrived.

As I write this, it almost seems I am repeating the histories of Lincoln and Churchill. All three of these great leaders anticipated the future and continually looked for the opportunity to strategically position themselves to be ready for the moment it arrived.

When offered freedom from prison in February 1985, in exchange for renouncing violence and the armed struggle by the South African Prime Minister P. W. Botha, Mandela refused feeling that it would be a betrayal of his principles and a betrayal of his people. It was a month later that Mikhail Gorbachev succeeded Konstantin Chernenko as Soviet Premier which precipitated the collapse of the Soviet Union. Prior to these events, South Africa had been strategically important to the Western world, but all this changed with the political changes in the East Bloc countries.

There was great strategy in this decision and with his willingness to spend the rest of his life behind bars, strengthened his position as a powerful symbol within the ANC, South Africa and around the world.

This was not an arbitrary decision, made out of spite or maliciousness. It was carefully and meticulously planned by a thoughtful and fertile mind. South African and world business leaders, as well as many previously 'friendly' nations took notice of this personal sacrifice and began to increase the pressure on the government of the time. Mandela, unlike the governments political leadership, could see over the horizon and the political, social and business changes that were beginning to take place as well as the impact of those changes and positioned himself accordingly.

He had an ever present dream, vision and conviction that good would at some point prevail over bad and inspired most people in South Africa to believe in a better future. A vision of a better future than the present and he communicated that vision in such a way that he drew most people with him and dragged others along until they saw the reality as he saw it.

Mandela had an enormous capacity for forgiveness, reconciliation and compassion towards those who had wronged him, his family and his people. He showed the world what it was to forgive and to move on. He made his enemies friends with his disarming smile and quick wit.

However, he too understood his weaknesses and readily admitted his failures. He understood his imperfections and personal struggles and daily fought himself to overcome those things he perceived as holding him back. His greatest challenge lay in changing himself.

And in these things lay his greatness as a leader. Unafraid to challenge the norm, eager to forgive, ready to reconcile, desperate to communicate his vision of tomorrow and focused on becoming a better person while building leadership capacity in others.

While these three great leaders are not the only leaders we can learn lessons from, I have used them to illustrate the need for great leaders and the fact that great leaders are not special people, endowed with super-human qualities, but are ordinary people, who make extra ordinary efforts to achieve their dreams.

CHAPTER 2

Leading yourself –
The First Level of
Leadership!

"Nothing so conclusively proves a person's ability to lead others, as what they do from day to day to lead themselves."

Thomas J. Watson, former chairman of IBM.

While researching and teaching on leadership, as well as coaching and mentoring leaders, much of the material available is focused on the 'what' questions of leadership. That means they are focused on what leadership is and discussing the various theories I have briefly touched on in the previous chapter. Very few, however, focus on the 'how to' and even less on the 'why' questions of leadership. The research has generally focused on the theories themselves rather than on the practical implementation of those theories or the implications of a narrow theory based focus. It appears that too great an emphasis has been placed on, what I believe, to be the horizontal or competency development stage, without being balanced with the vertical, practical development stage of leadership as a whole or of leadership development in particular.

While the horizontal stage is critical to understanding leadership development, it is generally delivered by an 'expert' in a training environment or found in a book written from the same perspective and is relatively generic in its make-up. Most books and training material used in the leadership development environment generally seem to follow the same pattern and often come from similar sources. That is, authors and program developers using the same generic material and perpetuating the same discussions around the various theories.

This mostly includes a discussion about what the various theories of leadership are with an emphasis on the theory favoured by the author or trainer, a discussion about leadership styles again with a focus on the style best suited to the author or trainer and very little about the personal transformation needed for great leadership.

The vertical, practical stage of leadership development focuses on the leader as an individual and the personal transformation as the individual learns to lead themselves first and develops the habit of continual and ongoing transformation. This is the practical and emotional implementation of all that has been researched and learned.

Much of the literature gives the impression of leadership as a disembodied process, which if applied as prescribed will have 'guaranteed' definable outcomes. Often when reading leadership books I have almost been able to hear the doctor say, *"take 2 of these pills for 3 days and call me in a week if they don't work".* Many of the leadership programs, training seminars and lectures I have attended, have provided a great deal about a particular theory and very little in the way of the practical application or of personal transformation. If solutions or practical applications have been recommended or discussed, they have had very little use in my working environment.

As a result of this over emphasis on the horizontal development and of this disembodied process, I have seen many leaders and people in leadership roles struggle to adopt the theories they have been taught or have read about often with disastrous consequences.

The truth is that leadership is not a disembodied process with definable outcomes as it is not an exact science. It is in fact totally the opposite. While most of the leadership theories place people in boxes and suggest leaders act and respond in those boxes, leadership is without question an expression of the individual and the response of other unique individuals to your leading. There is simply no box into which we can place people, including leaders.

While there are skills and theories which apply to leadership, there can be no separation from you as an individual. Everything about you, your experiences, family background, culture, thoughts, education, etc, have an impact on your leadership as well as how people respond to your leadership. It is equally true regarding the people you are looking to lead. They are individuals, with a whole range of backgrounds, cultures, thoughts, emotions, education, etc and their response to you and your leading is as unpredictable as tomorrow.

It is with this in mind that the following chapters have been developed. We will consider how your personal transformation will impact on your leadership as well as how you can grow into leading teams and organisations and how this can lead you to developing other leaders around you.

In the previous chapter we looked at the need for great leaders. From here on we will look at the 5 levels of leadership and will focus on the 'how' and the 'why' of becoming a great leader and of great leadership. We will look at how to engage not only those who follow as a consequence of your role or function, but how to engage even those who may be hostile to your leadership. We will consider how to transform yourself into the kind of leader people want to follow even when they are not required to do so. We will understand the reality and impact of a vision on your leadership ability and how 'why' drives the 'how to'.

Level 1 - Self-Leadership

The greatest challenge to leadership is not lack of resources, information or a lack of skill, but rather a lack of individual personal development. Leadership, whether in a business, social or political context, can be and often is simultaneously challenging, frustrating, depressing, stimulating, exhausting, exciting, emotionally exhilarating and completely draining. As a result of all of these and a myriad of other factors you, as a leader, must work harder on yourself than you do on other people, the organisation, the strategy or the execution of strategy. Leading yourself will not only enhance your ability to lead others, but will cause people to want to follow you. Great leaders have a clear sense of this need to continually grow and develop all areas of their lives.

I have found, through interviews with and observation of great leaders, that the truth of successful leadership does not lie in the alignment of the stars or the planets, the methodologies of 'attracting' success, country of birth, ethnic origin, luck or any other external factor, but rather lie in the leaders' ability to understand themselves first and to continually improve and adapt their skills. It is in understanding yourself as an individual that leadership begins and, in fact, ends. Leadership does not begin with understanding or even acting on a theory, it begins with you. You will never become a great leader of men and woman unless you become a great leader of yourself.

While I have never been a massive fan of the typical SWOT analysis or the interpretations used by some leadership writers and trainers, developing a personal profile of yourself which includes an understanding of your strengths and your weaknesses, is a vital component to becoming a great leader. However, be aware that the largest challenge I have encountered with personal profiles and SWOT analysis, is they become pigeonholes for peoples which often steals from their individuality.

SWOT analysis, when done correctly and for the right reasons, can and often is a good process. The challenge is they are seldom done well, for the right reasons and very often done with a lack of understanding or enthusiasm. Too many SWOT analysis programs and interpretations are used to stereo-type individuals, making them bland, one dimensional cookie-cutter, cardboard cut-outs and missing the individual creativity and dynamism every individual brings to any environment.

Often people completing a SWOT analysis will do so feeling a certain level of duress or be in a stressful setting, meaning they may not answer all the questions in a way they would typically respond if relaxed and at ease, therefore skewing the results and the information provided by the analysis. I have read many of these results and my immediate thought has been one of hardly recognising the person in the information from the person I have personally met, particularly with regard to strengths and weaknesses.

I am not discounting a SWOT analysis, but am mentioning it here as an alert to the pitfalls of an over reliance on the outcomes. In fact, I would encourage everyone, leader or not, to do regular SWOT analysis which could be compared with a previous report. This would give you some idea of how you have changed and grown over a period of time.

Great leaders are constantly looking for ways in which they can become better tomorrow than they are today. They are intentional about their efforts to grow and develop the skills and habits which will help them become a better person and leader. A well designed and critical SWOT analysis could be a large part of that intentionality.

Audacious leaders understand the effects of their personal transformation on the organisation and on the people around them.

Nelson Mandela once said, *"One of the most difficult things is not to change society, but to change yourself."*

The skill in leading yourself rests in the art of understanding who you are, what you are capable of, what capacity you have, what your strengths and weaknesses are. It is understanding where you are now and where it is you want to go in the future. Leading yourself is having a well-defined sense of your personal influence over your own actions, words, thoughts and activities.

Leading yourself is the skill of developing from the inside out. It is simultaneously the process of being aware and understanding both your strengths and weaknesses. By mitigating the effects of your weakness and making the most of your strengths, you can be an example to those around you and to those who follow you. These are skills that take time and effort to develop as you will need to overcome the natural tendency of, *'If I want it done correctly, I must do it myself.'*

For many years, I have had a love/hate relationship with exercise and food. There have been times when I love food and hate exercise and other times where I love food and exercise in equal amounts.

It has been a very rare occasion and moment of extreme turmoil; where I have loathed both simultaneously. This rare experience has, however, never lasted very long! I have also never derived any pleasure from running or jogging and have always found most 'health foods' bland and unappealing. While I do enjoy having a good workout, work pressures often get in the way of a consistent appearance at my local gym. As a result of these issues, I have often in jest said, *"Round is a shape and I am in shape,"* never realising that this was likely the greatest stumbling block to leading myself!

However, I have recently made the decision to examine leading myself and look at the areas of my life, which needed attention. I realised that I had put on more than just a few pounds and was beginning to feel uncomfortable and a little embarrassed. I have had to decide whether the pleasure of the 'chocolate bar' outweighs the pain of discomfort or visa-versa. I decided I have to be a better self-leader, before I am able to write about or train leadership principles and skills. So I have taken the steps necessary for me to gain control over my weight and my fitness.

This is about self-control. And self-control is one of the cornerstone habits of leading yourself. However, it is not only self-control in the food you eat or don't eat. It affects all areas of your life, from eating habits to vocabulary and attitude.

Self-leadership is about understanding the impact of your actions, words, attitudes and thoughts on the future. While very few people consider, for example, the impact of their thoughts on their lives, on the people around them and on the organisation they may lead, great leaders are constantly aware of the impact of their thoughts. They take control of their thoughts and remove those that are untrue, unsubstantiated, negative, degrading, demeaning and destructive.

Great leaders also understand the impact of their words on those around them and on themselves. While growing up, I often heard the phrase, *"sticks and stones may break my bones, but words will never harm me."* I have discovered the opposite is in fact true. The words we use are the most constructive and destructive forces known to mankind. And once those words have been spoken, they can never be taken back! Our words have consequences whether we mean them or not. They can be misunderstood, misinterpreted, badly translated, badly delivered and badly received. Or they can be understood, correctly interpreted, well delivered and well received.

This is about the disciplines you put into daily action, not only as a leader, but in every aspect of life. The more disciplined you are, the more effective you will be as a leader and the more people will want to follow you. The fact is, changing yourself means effectively changing the future direction of your life and as a leader, potentially the future direction of your organisation.

Every truly great leader I have studied, read about or met has been a massive student of themselves. From Abraham Lincoln and Nelson Mandela to some of the business leaders I have worked with and interviewed over the past 25 years, I have seen great leaders work very hard at leading and growing themselves.

I have also noticed that great leaders consistently display certain fundamental habits which they seem to work at continually. These habits form the basis of their leadership and I have discovered that these are all learned habits.

The first of these habits is **self-reflection on perception, understanding or philosophy**.

Your perceptions, understanding or philo sophy of any circumstance, person, situation, etc are completely determined by what you have heard, seen and experienced over the span of your life to date. Your philosophy could also be called your guiding principles. These are the foundational beliefs you have and hold, to which determine your understanding of everything. As with every other person, these will be built on a collection of your entire life's experience. For example, your experience of leadership may be of a demanding, negative and demonstrative person who has unrealistic expectations. You will look at all leaders and people in leadership roles and judge them according to your philosophy and will make a determination regarding them as a leader based on those thoughts.

The primary aim of this book and the associated courses is behavioural change. The challenge I have found is while most focus on the changes necessary from an external perspective, very few if any, focus on the beliefs and values which drive those changes and will ensure they are sustainable changes. It is right here that many leadership courses fail as they focus on the external presentation of the leadership skill without challenging and changing the internal perspectives and values which will sustain the skills.

And it is these internal values and perspectives which differentiate the great from the 'also-rans.'

Your perspective, understanding or philosophy is your unique view on the world and is the lens through which you will filter all things. It is what shapes how you act and react toward people, how you speak with or to individuals, how you communicate your feeling and emotions. It will determine with whom you will connect and the opportunities you will chase or leave. Your perspective will determine those issues you are passionate about and those you care nothing for. It is what drives your motivation to succeed or to maintain the level you are at. And it will determine whether you become a great leader or not!

In his book, 'Start with Why', author Simon Sinek says, "People don't buy 'What' you do, they buy 'Why' you do it." While I understand what his point is and I agree, my personal experience leads me to believe it goes further. People buy YOU first, before they buy your WHY. Whether you are a director, manager, preacher, sales person, it does not matter. People buy you first and they buy you because of who you are. They buy you because you have caused them to trust you. Who you are and the trust that is found in you is determined by your philosophy or perspective. It is determined by what you believe. And it's your philosophy that will determine the 'why' of everything you do.

So how do you change your philosophy?

A 2012 study reported on the BMC Neuroscience [2] website showed that a critical region of the brain was activated during periods of self-reflection. This region, called the anterior cingulate cortex (ACC) according to the report, when activated can help leaders identify, develop and understand their values, assist with the development of strategic vision and goals as well as assist in implementing the action plans necessary for success.

You can begin this process by spending time evaluating your values, your goals and aspiration. Ask yourself some challenging questions and don't be afraid to be really honest about your answers. You could ask questions such as:

- What you believe and whether that belief is true and justified?

- Whether your values have driven your results to date?

- How those beliefs impact on those around you and on the opportunities you encounter every day?

- Ask yourself what the factors and forces are which determine your point of view or your guiding principles?

I recommend you begin with your personal values. These are the values which are central to who you are and should be so strongly held as not to be violated by anything or anyone. Most people in leadership roles have very little idea of what their personal values are or know how these impact on the people around them and on everything they do.

My own values and perspectives are derived from reading and

mediating on the bible and the wisdom it provides. It is here, that I have found the principles and values by which I conduct my life and my leadership. I use these principles and values as a filter through which everything must pass and I will not violate them.

It would be a good time to begin the process by making a list of the values you think a leader should aspire to have. Below is a short list I have created to help with the development of your list.

Some find it useful to ascribe a numerical value to each ranging from 1 – 5, with the 1 being the highest and 5 being the lowest. No matter which methodology you use, determine the 5 core values which you aspire to.

Honesty	Work/Life Balance	Creativity
Integrity	Accountability	Ethical
Justice	Independence	Change
Love	Collaboration	Economic security
Loyalty	Friendship	Influence
Competency	Health	Recognition
Authority	Competition	Humor
Self-respect	Autonomy	Courage
Harmony	Wisdom	Self-Discipline

The purpose of beginning with your personal values is that you are firstly an individual, with emotions, thoughts, perceptions, etc, before you are a leader. Who you are will massively impact how you lead. While this may appear on the surface to be very basic, it is in fact the base on which all great leadership is built. Your personal values will determine how you respond to people and situations and they will affect your behaviour under pressure and in stressful situations.

Much has been written by philosophers and researcher over the past 150 years about the effects of your personal philosophy and values on your leadership style and effectiveness. I have found the ancient wisdom, 'As a man thinks in his heart, so he becomes,' [3] to be as true today as when it was written over 3000 years ago.

As you work through this list in order to determine these 5 core values, it would be important to answer some of the following questions. Again ask yourself the really hard questions and be clear and honest with yourself. It is after all for your benefit:

• What do I believe about myself?

• What do I believe about people?

• What do I believe about life?

- What do I believe about what it takes to create an effective organisation?

- Do my values align with the results I want from life?

Having completed this process of determining your personal values, you have also begun the process of developing your leadership values. As you begin to understand these values, you may have begun to change your perspective or philosophy, which is the first step in becoming a great leader through learning to lead yourself.

As you build your leadership philosophy through these values, I suggest you begin formulating a compelling vision which is driven by a significant purpose. In other words, where do you want to take your life and career and how will you want that to impact on your family, your friends, your organisation and your community. A significant purpose is something more than money in the bank, a big house or a sports car. These are potential upsides of having a compelling vision, but will not drive a true leader for very long.

Life and leadership has to be about something bigger.

For me it is about what the money I earn can do for my family, people less fortunate and for animals who have been abused. The specifics of these scare me, and drive me to do everything I can do to make them a reality. Having a significant vision can make you unstoppable.

Self-reflection and changing of your philosophy or perspective, will result to a change in your attitude.

This is the 2nd habit I see in great leaders. They work on having a **great attitude**.

While in the air force in the 1980's, I encountered a number of leaders and leadership styles. Many of the leaders I encountered were leaders as a consequence of their function, rank and/or position. For obvious reasons a rank structure in a military context is important and should be strictly, but not abusively, observed. The challenge, however, is that many people within military structures, promoted to leadership roles have little to no idea of what leadership is and as a result their leadership style is based on fear and abuse. For example, many junior officers gain their rank as a result of an educational qualification and a simple officers course, but lack any real understanding of leadership nor have developed the skills needed to lead troops in combat.

From my 6 and a half years' experience in the military, 2 'leaders' remain vividly in my mind. Flight Sergeant 'Blackie' Swarts* and Sergeant Andre Saunders*. Two men with vastly contrasting styles and consequently, contrasting results. Blackie Swarts was a quietly spoken, patient and considerate man, who drew those in his team in from the very first time anyone met him. He was almost instantly trustworthy and likeable. In stark contrast was Andre Saunders. He was arrogant, loud, foul-mouthed and completely self-absorbed. Not the kind of person many people wanted to befriend or trust.

I vividly remember arriving on my first day at the air force base, knowing no one, feeling completely out of place and the first person I encountered was Sergeant Saunders and my experience with his brand of leadership began. As his new apprentice, I was informed, I was a lower form of life than anything on the ocean floor, had no reason for existing other than reasons he provided and was to be available immediately at his call. Fortunately, Saunders had only been left in charge of the workshop while Blackie Swarts was on leave and so to my enormous relief, he returned 2 days later.

I could not believe the difference in leadership and the atmosphere in the workshop. The greatest change was in Andre's demeanour. Subdued and apparently mild-mannered while Blackie was around, a tyrant when he wasn't. And to my further relief, I was not to be his apprentice! Over the following 12 months, I watched as Blackie Swarts absorbed book after motivational book and worked on developing himself and accepting responsibility, while Andre spent his time shifting blame for all his bad decisions and looking for praise for the efforts of those who had the misfortune to form a part of his team. Blackie had the ability to help each person in his team see the possibilities and move toward them. He seemed to want individuals to grow and to becoming all they could possibility be. Andre was focused on holding everyone back and keeping them below him. He despised anyone who advanced, while Blackie promoted everyone's advancement.

A few years later, I had occasion to discuss both leaders with a mutual acquaintance, who at the time was a colonel and had known both men for many years. His response summed the 2 individuals up perfectly.

> *"If you give a small man great power, he remains a small man. But give a small man with a desire to change himself great power and he will become a great man."*

The difference in the attitude of both men toward everything was totally contrasting and was reflected in everything they did and said. The more Blackie read and reflected on his own leadership abilities and skills, the more these skills developed and he changed and the more people followed him without being asked. The effect of this change was reflected in his attitude toward himself, his job, those in his team, his peers and his superiors. We all felt the effects and most of us began to develop similar habits. In fact, had it not been for his influence, it is highly unlikely that I would not be where I am today nor would I have written this book.

Becoming a leader can be hard and being a great leader even harder. With the wrong attitude you will make your leadership experience more challenging and people will find it increasingly difficult to follow you.

The fact is, attitude is contagious and this is particularly true for a leader. The question is, 'would anyone want to catch yours?' How often do you have an attitude check? Author John Maxwell said, *'People hear your word, but they feel your attitude.'*

I know it is a cliché, however, your attitude does determine your altitude. This is the level at which you function and the level at which your leadership impacts people, teams and organisations. Understanding that your attitude is one of the most controllable and changeable areas of your life. The ability to understand, it is not what happens to you that should determine your attitude, but rather the way in which you choose to think and respond to circumstances, people, issues, etc, that will determine and will reveal your attitude. Many people in leadership roles allow their past negative experiences to determine their attitude, instead of allowing their philosophy to be the determining factor.

The fact is, your philosophy determines your attitude and it determines the impact you will have on circumstance and people over time. It will also determine your actions or activity.

And this leads to the 3rd habit I have seen in great leaders. Great leaders **take bold action** even when it hurts.

Taking bold action does not mean that great leaders are arrogance, reckless or even careless in the actions they take. It does mean that they are willing to take the most appropriate action for the circumstances and if required, will not hesitate to take the action that others will not take.

You see, courage is one of the most important qualities a leader can possess. It is the quality, along with trust, that will cause people to rally around the leader in challenging times and the quality which will cause a leader to step up and step forward no matter what the odds are. Like leadership itself, courage or boldness in leadership is a quality that can be learned and developed by anyone. And like any habit, the more it is practiced, the easier it becomes.

It has always amazed me, while observing leaders, how the more they put themselves in the game, the more success they have. Those that stand back and are afraid of stepping up are equally less successful. And yes, it sounds obvious and easy, but if it was so obvious and easy, why don't we have more great leaders?

Courage to take bold action will also cause you to hang in until it works out. And I have observed that the really courageous and bold leaders hang in through the tough times until the rainbow appears and all the clouds blow away. Boldness generally produces tenacity and an unwillingness to give up.

And finally, the willingness to take bold action, will cause you to be unconstrained by the past and its failures and it will lead you to be innovative and inventive. The fact is the future is owned by the bold, the innovative and the inventive. Bold leaders take risks and generally win.

The 4th habit I have noticed is that great leaders are **excellent listeners**.

Great leaders are great listeners. I believe that leaders who don't listen well will very soon find themselves surrounded by people who have very little, if anything to contribute to any conversation. It is very easy to impresse people by your eloquent speech, however, you will have a greater impact and influence if you impress them by your ability to listen.

I will never forget a particular discussion I had with a wonderful pastor of a church on the outskirts of the city. Although I did not know him as well as I would have like to, Trevor Yoko taught me many gems about life, people and business. *"If you want people to see you as a leader,"* he said, *"always remember you were blessed with 2 ears and one mouth. It may be that the message is in the design."*

To become a great leader, you will need to learn the skill of using your ears for more than just hearing, which I describe as a passive activity, but for listening, which I believe is an active process. While I'm not an audiologist or hearing professional, I believe there is a distinction between hearing and listening.

During your day, you will hear many things. A telephone may ring in another office, cars and buses may pass your office, a baby may cry while you are walking the dog. All of these you hear, but don't have to actively do anything. The sound is there. Although you may hear the sounds you don't have to actively participate in them, respond to them or even remember them. This is hearing. A passive activity. It is however, how most people 'listen', which is one reason why misunderstandings occur. I'm sure you've heard the phrase, *'You're not listening to me'*? This question is generally a result of a person hearing passively, while constructing in their mind what they believe the solution, answer or point should be.

Listening on the other hand requires active participation. Listening is a skill that can be learned but it requires effort and a desire to understand. Leaders who listen well and do not just hear are leaders who become influential and are able to show empathy and sincere caring. When you as a leader listens, you will reduce misunderstandings, disagreements and generally you will save time and money. When a leader listens, it is with the intention of gaining understanding of the speakers' perspective, need and question.

Great leaders have an intentionality about their listening and concentrate to ensure they fully understand, even when receiving feedback about themselves. In order to listen well, as a leader you will need to learn to talk less.

A few years ago, I worked with a client who owned a consultancy based in Lincoln. Toby was an entrepreneur, who was always chasing the next 'shiny' thing which could make him bags of money. He had the potential to be a really good leader, but was held back by his inability to listen to what other people were saying. He had very strong preconceived ideas and entrenched views about most issues and would almost shut down during any conversation as he thought he already knew the answer or solution.

I recall one particular conversation, if it could be called that, in which having started to explain an issue to him, noticed a 'look' on his face. I knew he was no longer listening, instead was formulating his answer in his mind before understanding the context or the resolution. At that point, while continuing to relate the issue, I switched to speaking in Afrikaans, a language he neither spoke nor understood. When I stopped speaking, Toby provided answers that were totally unrelated to what I had been explaining. He could never understand why his clients, business partners and staff were always at odds with him.

The great leaders I have met and spoken with seem to have developed the ability to listen to your words as well as 'read between the lines' of the people they work with, clients and generally most people they come across. But the ability to understand is closely linked to the ability or skill of listening. Listening with intention will lead to a greater level of understanding and will prevent misunderstanding.

However, understanding does not just come from listening to the words that are spoken, but also from considering the motivations, back story and the individual speaking. Great leaders listen with the intention of gaining an understanding, whether they agree with the speaker or not. Agreement is irrelevant to the skill of listening for a great leader. It has to do with understanding and it is only through understanding that a leader can redirect or gain new insight that they may not previously have had.

This desire to understand leads into the 5th habit which is an understanding of the need to **connect with people** at more than a superficial level.

As a leader, connecting with people at a level deeper than 'hello' or 'hope you are well', is an integral part of building trust and of developing your authority to lead. Irrespective of your personality type, building relationships through connecting with the people around you and in your team is a must for any leader. It is the people whom you have connected with who will have your back when things don't work out.

It is also the leaders who reach out to their team or allow others to reach toward them, who are the most effective in leadership.

During my 6 years in the military, I encountered a wide array of leadership style, methods, attitudes and saw the worst as well as occasionally the best example of leadership. I have already mentioned a few examples, but the best example I saw of connecting was during a particular time of personal challenge. I was stationed at AFB Port Elizabeth, when a set of personal circumstances arose back home in Durban, approximately 1000 km away. I wanted a transfer to AFB Durban to be closer to home so I could manage the situation. Despite numerous transfer requests, both written and verbal, through the regular channels, as well as some irregular channels and a vacancy at the base, no-one seemed in the slightest bit interested in acknowledging my request, much less approving it.

As the situation became more desperate and urgent, I took every opportunity that came my way to put my case to the senior ranks at the base and at headquarters. Everything changed though, when the Chief of the Air Force Gen Muller and the Sergeant Major of the Air Force Barry Kemp, visited the base. I had noticed that Kemp was taking time to chat with everyone and seemed to be completely absorbed by each conversation. He listened and asked questions and in a few cases took individuals aside for a more private chat.

Not thinking he would do anything different from those I had already spoken to, I explained my situation when he came over to me. Immediately, Kemp took me into a nearby office and we discuss the situation for over an hour. He asked detailed questions about the situation in particular, but also about my background and what I wanted to achieve in the future. Finally, someone was willing to listen and understand. He showed genuine empathy and consideration, never once condemning or appearing to be condescending.

While in the office, he made a few phone calls and before the end of the day, my transfer was approved and the orders were posted. That evening I flew home and the next morning reported to my new base. A few months later, he was on an inspection tour of AFB Durban and specifically sort me out and had a private conversation with me to ensure that everything was being done to resolve the situation at home.

While on a business trip a few years after I had left the Air Force, I bumped into Barry. Although some time had elapsed and he had retired, Barry instantly recognised me and we spent a fair amount of time talking about the issue and the consequences which stemmed from it.

Barry Kemp connected with me in a way that no one else had. He took the time to understand me and the circumstance. As he got to know me, he knew it was not a scam nor was I looking for an easy ride. He was able to make a judgement call with all the facts. I consider Barry Kemp to be a great leader.

Conversely, while working for ABSA Bank, the senior leaders of the organisation would often, during conferences and meetings, give long speeches about their open door policy and their approachability. The fact is, during the 2 years I worked at the bank, I never had anything approaching a conversation with any of the senior managers and actually had more contact and greater discussions after I had left than I had while I was working for the bank. This problem was not restricted to the board or the heads of departments, but existed as far down the ladder as the regional managers.

It was an open door in name, but a closed, iced over door in practice. And I believe it was one of the major contributing factors to the failure of the division. Looking back, I could not with any honesty recognise any of those managers faces or names and certainly would not consider any of them to be leaders.

Connecting with your team, irrespective of its size, will help you to understand them. Understand how they generally react to stress, pressure, deadlines, workflow challenges and personality clashes. You will know when they need privacy, encouragement, a laugh or a strong, guiding hand. Employees in today's market place, want leaders to be more mindful of their emotional, mental, personal and physical needs. They want to be recognised for who they are, not just a number or what they do and the leader who recognises this fact will build stronger bonds with their team.

A large part of leadership is found in the individuals' ability to motivate and influence a group of people to achieve a goal or vision. And connecting with you team, plays no small part in developing and maintaining this ability to motivate and influence. Not everyone is motivated in the same way and without connecting with each person in your team individually, you will not understand how to motivate or encourage them.

It takes time and effort, but wisely getting to know each person individually over time, will be of enormous benefit to you as the leader and to the team in general. Taking steps to understand their likes and dislikes, hobbies, sports affiliation, TV favourites is a good place to begin. This is an easy and non-threating starting point and can gain you massive trust and respect if handled correctly.

Coming in as the interim CEO of BCR Associates, I had to build a relationship with the team who had worked with the major shareholder and previous CEO for many years. I focused on getting to know each individual as a separate from the business. Mike, for example, is a Manchester United fan and I am a Liverpool fan and so we chatted football on a regular basis, with a whole load of banter thrown into the mix. We spent time discussing family issues, which helped me understand when he needed time off for family reasons, without question.

It developed a relationship, which stood up to a number of challenging situation which arose. Including a time when I suspended his best friend from the business. Even now, having moved on from the business, we are still in communication and regularly discuss football.

Conversely, the financial manager would not allow a relationship of trust to develop with anyone and was consequently never seen as a part of the team. It made trusting her extremely difficult and conversations, even at a social level, were never pleasant. When the business needed to be restructured, she was not seen as integral to the team or the operation of the business and was released.

Connecting is a two-way street, but you as the leader must work hard at connecting as deeply as possible with the individuals in your team as the team coalesces and develops.

By connecting with your team, you will develop the authority to lead, motivate and influence them leading you directly into the 2nd level of the 5 levels of great leadership.

CHAPTER 3

Leading Teams - The Second Level of Leadership.

"The task of leadership is not to put greatness into humanity, but to elicit it, for the greatness that is already there."

— John Buchan

'Leaders must forget about B2B or B2C and focus on P2P. Person to person. This is the strength of team development.'

Vic Williams

Level 2 – Developing and leading a team

If leading yourself is the first level in becoming a great leader, the second stage has to be understanding, developing and leading a team of people effectively. And to be great at developing a team, you have to become the person others choose to follow. Hence, the reason this level follows leading yourself.

100

It is important to remember at the beginning of this discussion on team leadership, that it does not matter whether the 'team' consists of one other person, a hundred people or ten thousand people, the principles of team leadership remain the same. It is simply a matter of scale and scalability. If the fundamentals on which you construct, develop and lead your team are not scalable, your team will not be scalable going forward and failure will be the result.

The assumption is often that, by sending people on a management or leadership course, including an accredited course, promoting them to a leadership role and giving them a title of manager or director, they will become leaders and other people in subordinate roles will follow their every instruction with enthusiasm and a team will develop! This is just an illusion. A course, diploma, degree, PhD, will never make a leader. These may provide some tools, but it cannot in any way be suggested, they produce leaders. In the same way that leaders are not born, courses, universities and colleges can't produce leaders. They can provide skills and ideas, but not leaders.

The fact is, if you do not connect with the people in your 'team' at a person to person level and do not develop into the type of person they want to follow, they will often do the most irrational things and will find ingenious ways to prevent your success as a leader and will resist you all the way, irrespective of the consequences.

Rajen Pillay was a long time employee of a large, international hydraulics company. The company had called me in to work with a newly promoted sales manager, John in one of their local offices. John had attended a one-year management course which consisted mainly of weekly night classes at a local college and had done a number of supplemental management training day courses, including a sales management specific course. He had previously been a high performing salesmen with over 6 years' experience with the company, was well known by the regions clients and had great product knowledge.

The idea of senior management at the company was, he had the education, the knowledge, it should be perfect! Promote John, give him the regional sales manager title, an office with a great view of a nearby golf course, a better company car and an expense account. What could possibly go wrong? By the time I was called in, half of his direct reports were looking for other jobs outside of the company and two had already left.

John was applying all the management principles he had been taught, but everything was going horribly wrong. When he needed to be a leader, he could only be a manager. He set and managed targets, read call reports, developed systems and processes to know where all of his reports were at any time and blamed his 'poor' quality sales team for the declining results, just as he had seen his superiors do for years.

Rajen, I soon discovered, thought he should have received the promotion to sales manager. He had been at the company longer than John, had performed at the same level and was older and, in his mind, wiser than John. When the announcement was made, Rajen's only thought and focus was to see John's demise and had set about doing all he could to undermine John's authority and get people to see him as the right person for the job. He spread stories of a funding crisis and restructuring in the business, of job losses and due to John not focusing on building relationships with those in the group, everyone began accepting he was holding the 'party' line. He focused everyone who would listen on John's short comings and on the falling sales.

We discovered that instead of these sales people working on their client base, they were meeting Rajen at coffee shops to discuss the 'situation'. John lost their respect and trust, which led to colleagues looking for other jobs and some actually leaving. Although it ultimately cost Rajen his job, he persisted with his irrational, unpredictable behaviour for the next 6 weeks.

After working with John once a week for 8 weeks, he had turned this group of individuals around, Rajen had been dismissed and a team was beginning to form. It took another 7 months of hard work for John, but eventually it turned the corner and within 2 years it was the top performing team in the company. Over a period of time, John had discovered that team building has less to do with qualifications, titles or managing call reports and everything to do with person to person interaction.

I have often asked people in training courses, seminars or during one-to-ones to describe the words team and teamwork and have consistently found similar thought processes irrespective of the audience or the country. In well over 85% of cases, individuals begin explaining teamwork from the perspective of a sports team they either follow or have been influenced by or from an experience they have had in a military context.

It has been a very rare occasion that anyone has given me a definition of either word that does not involve a long explanation surrounding the above mentioned sports or military connection. And even more rarely do I have anyone attempt to describe their office or place of work as a definition of team or team work. Approximately 7% of people whom I have asked this question, used their workplace to describe teamwork and although over 90% have spoken as being part of a team, only 3% used that 'team' to describe the word team.

While these numbers have no empirical research or detailed study to back them up, they are observations I have made and noted over approximately 20 years, I have asked why this is?

Why do so few people use their work place or, if they are a manager or supervisor, their own 'team' as a definition of team or teamwork? Is it because so few people actual believe they work in a real team? Or is there a lack of understanding regarding what a team should look like? Or has the word become synonymous for *any* group of people working in a given space or on a specific project?

I think the latter question is most likely the truth. We so often hear managers talk about the group of people who report to them as, 'their team' or senior executives speak of their employees in general as 'the team', that the words and implications have become almost ubiquitous and honestly, worthless. It has become one of those flippant phrases or corporate buzzwords which imply something expected of a group of people in a work environment. It has been thrown in with words like, core competency, buy-in, empower and 'think outside the box'. All are good leadership and management concepts, but so last year as a result of over use, mainly by MBA graduates, consultants and ignorance.

The perception is, throw a group of people together to work on a common issue and by calling them a team, they will act like one. Unfortunately, the reality is so far removed from this perception as to make most of these groups less than successful and very often they fail in doing what they were established to do. This is a fact with all types of 'teams' in all types of environments. From sales and management to scientific and educational, groups of people don't simply become a team by default, no matter how much we wish it would happen and no matter how many team building exercises managers arrange or seminars they attend. Team building and development is far more complex and requires constant effort to make and keep it a reality.

So what then are Teams and how do you establish Teamwork

An understanding of how teams work or don't work, how they develop and how to manage the variety of teams and team functions is critical to successful leadership. Great leaders learn and refine the skills required for building great teams and then replicate that over and over again. And while this may seem simplistic and obvious, we have a global leadership crisis as mentioned earlier in this book and one of the most effective ways of overcoming this crisis is for leaders to grow the skills of leadership, including the skill of team building.

Before we look at some fundamentals for building a great team, let me emphasis this fact. There is no 'one-size-fits-all' rule book to team building and team work, just as there is no one-size-fits-all leadership rule book. There are a few fundamentals which can help, but as I discussed earlier, we are dealing with humans, who, like yourself are notoriously unpredictable. You will have people in your group that will want mountains of proof before moving in any direction on one project and on the next, when you think you will have a real battle on your hands, will go with you and will be the biggest advocate of the project.

Not everything you think is a 'no-brainer' will be to the people in your group or team. Some people will need to be inspired, encouraged and pumped up and others will be 'yes' men and women irrespective of the project or possible outcomes. It is important, if you are to build a great team, that you not only understand these facts, but that you come to terms with them and work with them instead of against them.

In the introduction I spoke about understanding the why before understanding the how or the what of leadership. It is what this book is focused on.

So why do we need to develop great teams? What are the benefits to the company, the community, the nation?

There is an interesting piece of research work done by the Royal Veterinary College at the University of London, reported on the 15th January 2014 on the website nature.com, studying the flying patterns of endangered northern bald ibises, which illustrates a part of the answer.

A flock of 14 hand reared birds were fitted with data loggers, which included GPS and accelerometers. The research confirmed a long known fact regarding the team work of large winged birds and discovered a previously unknown fact in the process. It appears that not only do the birds fly in the correct position to save energy, but by timing the flapping of their wings to synchronise with the bird ahead of them they also take advantage of the vortex created by the wings of the bird ahead.

What this research illustrates is not only the importance of teamwork in achieving greater results, but it also illustrates a number of the factors which impact the development of great teams, which I will discuss later in this chapter.

As mentioned earlier, most people will describe a sports team or a military experience when asked to define the words team or teamwork. As a sports fan and having spent 6 years in the military, I can relate to this way of defining teamwork, as there have been very few experiences in my working career where the business I have worked for or with could be described as a team or in fact, in many case, even having a team within the organisation.

In this context, one of the best examples of team work I have seen was the Liverpool Football Club teams from 1963 through 1985. While they undoubtedly had some great players at the time who could have played in almost any team then and now, the likes of Emlyn Hughes, Kevin Keegan, Phil Neal, Ray Clemence, Ian St John, Roger Hunt, Kenny Dalglish and Ian Rush, for the most part they were good players who played at the best level they could resulting in the sum of the parts being greater than the individuals. They played for each other and accomplished more than most could ever dream of. In most circumstances, when each of the individual players played for their respective countries, they were not nearly as effective as when they played for Liverpool.

I have seen the same team ethic in a number of other great sports teams, for example, Manchester United under Sir Alex Ferguson, Barcelona managed by Pep Guardiola, the Green Bay Packers of the Favre era and the 2015 Mercedes Formula 1 pit crew and, as a golfer (occasional hacker actually) who could forget the team work of the European Ryder Cup team of 2012.

The so-called 'miracle of Medinah', where thousands of Americans and a hand full of European golf fans came together to see if the American team could claw back the cup they had lost 4 years earlier. The tournament, held every 2 years, pitted the best male players from America against the best players from Europe since 1927. Over that time, the galleries had seen some incredible golf played at the highest level by fierce but fair competitors, who not only wanted to entertain, but wanted to win.

They had witnessed Jack Nicklaus concede to Tony Jacklin at Royal Birkdale in 1969, ensuring the tournament was tied and had experienced Bernhard Langer's missed putt on the last hole at Kiawah Island in 1991 handing the title to the Americans and had witnessed Darren Clarke's raw emotions at the K Club in 2006. But never before had a team so shown its strength and fight as at Medinah.

On days 1 and 2, the Americans forged ahead into a lead most thought was unassailable, except that is, for the European players, particularly Ian Poulter who almost single-handedly kept Europe in the game. 10-6 down at the beginning of day 3, it seemed a lost cause. If this was just a group of people working together and not a team with passion to succeed, they would have packed it in and gone home.

The American players and their supporters were in full cry, noisily proclaiming the impressive array of players in their team and in total expectation of celebrating come the end of the day and the end of the tournament. But it wasn't to be. The question that arises is, were they, the American's that is, a team or just a collection of great players presented as a team? I think the latter. The most obvious fact is these players played for themselves, their individual celebrity and celebrated as individuals not as a team.

This European group of players, by contrast, played as a team. With everything against them, including the fact they were playing in America, with an overwhelmingly large percentage of the crowd against them and most of the American player ranking higher than the Europeans, they should have lost. It was a hopeless cause, but they were inspired, motivated and cajoled by each other, their captain and the vice-captains to a win, a tournament which has become known as the miracle of Medinah.

And in this story, are the keys to developing a great team. For those who don't play or understand golf, it is a highly individualistic sport, particularly at the professional level. Each person playing for themselves with the individual aim of winning and the more a player wins the higher their world ranking. I think it was Tiger Woods who said, 'Second place is first loser' and that is the general professional golfer's mentality. Nothing wrong with it and nothing right with it. That is the way it is!

And yet, here were 12 individuals who spend most of their time playing for themselves and focused on personal performance, welded together as a team to achieve one of team sports greatest victories ever.

How did they do it? What were the fundamentals at work here?

While there are many factors that influence the definition and development of any team, these can, in general, be distilled down to 5 basic factors or fundamentals, all of which I see were at work in the European team of 2012.

Simply organising a group of likeminded people together, even if they are organised around a common goal, does not make a team. Neither does the so called 'feel good' factor come close to describing or defining a team and there is this unspoken myth that by using the word 'team,' everyone involved will somehow, magically come together and instantly be a team!

Some of these, for example, like mindedness and having a common goal, are important dynamics which develop over time within a great team, but are not the defining factors of a great team. The fact is, that even in a great team some people pull in different directions and there will be people who do not like their team mates, but respect and trust them enough to make the team dynamic work. There may not even be a feel good factor.

One of the best teams I ever worked with was a group of people who did not really like each other, but together were absolutely dynamic. We outsold not only the competitors, but the other sales teams in the company as well. We were all so unlike each other and thought in totally opposite directions, but it worked. Again the 5 basic factors that I describe below were at work in this group.

The first of these fundamentals in developing a great team is for you as the leader to have a good idea of where you are going with your life and career, where you would like to take this group of people and what it is you would like to see them accomplish and become. This is your why. It all starts right here and will die right here too.

This is often called a vision and all great leaders have a plan of how they see that vision becoming a reality. If you have a clear vision for your life and of where you want to take your fledgling team, you will begin this team building process in a really strong and confident position.

It is often said that if you own your vision, then you can get people to 'buy-in' to it. This term 'buy-in' is one of those over used and annoying management terms that worked in the 20th Century but has lost its impact and, I believe, its application in the 21st Century. It also gives the impression of inflexibility and arrogance on the part of the manager. Buy-in communicates, 'accept it or go away' and that's hardly great leadership.

A vision for where you are going and how you are getting there is not for people to buy-in to. Rather it is for people to see and understand that you are serious about your future. Your vision should allow you to accept the input of those around you and be open to questioning. This will help make your vision stronger, more believable and will give people reason, even if some disagree with you, to follow you.

Think of Nelson Mandela or Clement Attlee. Both had a vision of the future and knew where they wanted to take their respective countries and yet had people very close to them in total disagreement with that destination. Mandela did not only have to convince the population of the country, but he had to convince the members of his own party that a free country was possible. Some of his strongest critics were those closest to him and yet they followed because of his dream.

The same is true for Attlee, who despite the continual threat from his rivals in the post war Labour party, has been recognised as Britain's greatest 20th century Prime Minister ahead of Winton Churchill, by a poll of university academics. He sold them on his dream of a better Britain to the extent that the political manifesto promises were fulfilled quickly and efficiently, even by those who disagreed with the manifesto promises.

Both men were confident enough to leave themselves open to challenge and allowed those suggestions and arguments to shape their vision and eventually see it become a reality. They both knew where they were going, how they were going to get there and lived their dream.

The 2nd of these fundamentals is that the group must accept and share mutual responsibility and accountability for the delivery of the shared and clearly defined goal or goals. Although it is the leader of the group who is ultimately responsible, teams succeed and fail together. Success or failure must be the responsibility of the leader for a group of people to truly be called a team.

Like most people, I have often heard business and sports leaders shift the blame for failure to other people or to their team, rather than accepting responsibility. A quick look back at 2007/8 and the financial mess the world was in, saw fingers pointed from the top down and in all directions except at the culprits and realise that no-one has ever been prosecuted for causing that mess. Politicians and business leaders alike casting blame at everything and everyone, except themselves. From Gordon Brown, Alistair Darling, Mervyn King and Matt Ridley to Alan Greenspan, Ben Bernanke, Dick Fuld and Angelo Mozilo, have blamed others, but none have accepted their responsibility for the decisions they made which led to the financial mess which is still being felt today.

A few years ago, I was approached by the directors of an SME in Bristol to help them resolve the issues they had in their business. They were struggling to develop the business and had finally agreed to get external help. I listened with growing interest and amazement as each of the directors deflected blame to everyone else in their department and to other members of the board during my initial discovery meeting. The finger pointing and lack of responsibility was about average for what I see on a regular basis in boardrooms around the country. They had absolutely no trust in each other and it immediately became apparent the main culprit was Raymond, the MD and majority shareholder.

He blamed everyone, for everything, relentlessly. He accepted absolutely no responsibility for anything, even for the wrong decisions he had made. Consequently, none of his staff had much trust in him, the directors, the management or in fact in each other. Throughout the business it was the same story. It was and still is a great business, with a great product range, enormous potential and some really great people, but was being destroyed by the blame game. No one on the board took responsibility for failure and there was no accountability to each other. That the company had lasted 10 years was a minor miracle.

When we had finally got everyone, particularly Raymond, to understand the problem, its effects on the business and how to deal with it, the business slowly became a better place to work for everyone. Nowhere near being great or the finished article, each of the directors has a challenging road to travel and some may not last, but the progress has been great to see.

The third of these factors is that the individuals in the team need to be interdependent on each other's skills, talents and abilities. A group of people all with the same skills will generally all look at an issue, problem or challenge from the same perspective. The same would be true for a group of likeminded people. Perspectives have the tendency of becoming one-dimensional rather than multi-faceted. Narrow rather than innovative.

In early 2014, I had the great privilege of facilitating the merger of 3 fairly large medical practices. Having done other mergers previously, I understood the process and the requirements, so although I knew there would be challenges, I was comfortable with what needed to be done. The partners from the various practices were, in general, way out of their depth and comfort zones, but each brought different skills, talents and abilities to the table. We had people with very strong opinions and others who were passive/submissive. There were, of course, people who had been managing partners who suddenly were not. There were young, new partners and individuals who had been partners for many years.

What I found amazing, however, was how over a few months of coaching and challenging, each of these partners began to understand and value each other and although not always in agreement, they worked and continue to work together. It was refreshing to work with a group of people who understood what they did not know and were willing to learn and develop new skills.

Was it easy for them? Certainly not. There were major personality clashes and disagreements about policies, processes, staffing requirements and just about every other issue you could think of. But the partners had a will to make it work and that meant they had to change and grow as individuals.

Are they perfect? No. Do they now agree with each other? No. But they have developed into a team. It has taken time and effort and certainly not been a bed of roses. The COO, Claire, who came into the practice brought some amazing skills, which the business needed and have complimented the partners perfectly. They are inter-dependent on each other for success.

The 4th factor is communication. Right here is where most team building fails miserably. Communication is not a 1-way deal. It is the ability to listen, discuss, argue, disagree, agree and think through issues, challenges and options without personalities becoming involved or being negatively affected. This must include the confidence to honestly and realistically evaluate each other's performance and provide constructive feedback, without diminishing the other person's value or their contribution.

Great communication is not only what you say, but more importantly how you say it. The intonation, which can indicate attitude and emotion as well as the inflection of your voice, which can convey your mood and the words you chose to use, determine the value and effect of your communication. The same words spoken with a different tone and conveyed with the right attitude, will build rather than destroy. Will encourage and motivate rather than discourage and demotivate.

Communication within the team should also focus more on listening with the aim of understanding and speaking to be understood. Generally, communication is seen as a top down process. The manager says and everyone is expected to understand and do. This does not make for an effective team. An effective team is all about collaboration and contribution, through the skill of communication.

The 5th factor has to do with the size of the team. When it comes to sports teams, we know the size of the team will be subject to the rules of the particular sport in which the team participates. Soccer and cricket, for example, have 11 on field players, baseball have 9 and basketball have 5. Some sports allow replacement players, like rugby or have different offensive and defensive teams, like American football.

Although there are no such rules for business, social, community and political teams, there are guidelines based on research which show the optimal size of an effective team. It almost goes without saying, the bigger the team, the easier it is for some people, who may be less vocal, confident or less able to communicate well, to get 'lost' in the crowd. As I have interacted with teams of various sizes, in many different environments, I have noticed that larger teams, those over 15, tend to have more individual performance related issues than smaller, tighter teams.

My research seems to suggest that teams of 8-12 are the optimum size for the most productivity. Everyone has the opportunity to contribute and feel valuable. As far back as the 1860's, the question of team size has been asked and discussed from a variety of different perspectives. French agricultural engineer Maximilien Ringelmann's research, for example, showed that as more people become involved in a task, their individual performances decrease as each participant feels their contribution is less important and less critical. Known as the Ringelmanns Effect, its conclusions were added to by Alan Ingham and his colleagues at the University of Massachusetts Amherst.

Ringelmann's original experiment measured the effort of students in a simple rope pulling exercise, in which he found that 8 people did not pull as hard or as effectively as 4. Ingham and his colleagues replicated the experiment in the 1970's, but added a twist which led to a deeper understanding of team dynamics. They asked some of the student on the team to pretend to pull on the rope, while not actually doing the pulling. The conclusion from this experiment was that those actually pulling on the rope, pulled no harder than they had previously done when they and those told to pretend, were pulling together. It has become known as social loafing.

We can take a lesson from the bible. Jesus chose 12 disciples, all of whom were different in their character and personality, brought different skills and talents to the group and each of them were able to contribute and be valued, for good reason. This was not a random act, but a conscious and well thought out plan. He knew something most organisations miss when it comes to team building.

Considering lines of communication as a factor relating to the optimum size of a team, if the team consists of 6 people, you have 15 lines of communication. Increase that team to 12 and you don't double the lines of communication, but you more than quadruple to 66 lines of communication! The implications for leadership success are obvious and one of the main reasons why military units are broken down into small groups.

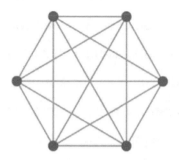

6 people, 15 lines

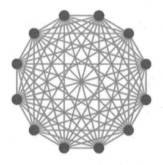

12 people, 66 lines

Team development

We have been talking about team building in general, but how do you go about picking a team that will function well together? How do you find the right blend of people? How do you work with a team that has been put together either by your predecessor or by the company and you have no control over the choices?

It is important to understand there are many different types of teams you may need to develop and lead with each type having its own dynamic requirements, along with skills and abilities to ensure the task is completed. You may, for example, need to form a sales team or a technical team. You will need to consider all the options and requirements of the job before looking for the right candidates to begin creating the team. This may seem obvious to some but certainly it is not to most in leadership roles.

The biggest challenge managers and leaders face, however, is not putting together 'their' own team, but rather inheriting an existing group of people or trying to lead one that has been dumped on them as a result of another 'leaders' failure. In these types of scenarios great leaders begin to build trust through the 5 fundamentals mentioned earlier.

Each individual will be trying to re-establish themselves within the group. By taking time to get to know and understand each person in the team and by sharing your vision with them individually and collectively, you will begin the process of building trust. And trust will cause them to follow and work with you.

It really does not matter whether you are starting a new team or taking over an existing one, you will need to make sure you have the right people, to do the right job, at the right time. You will need to choose carefully and with wisdom.

Raymond Meredith Belbin, a British researcher and management theorist, studied team work for many years and discovered that people tend to fall into or assume 'roles' within every team. He identified 9 different roles which seemed to exist within every team. People, his research showed typically fall into 2 or 3 roles where they may feel the most comfortable and prefer to work in, one or 2 others they will cover if required to do so and the rest they would prefer to stay well away from.

Again, I think it important to remind you that this is not an exercise of science or perfection. You are dealing with the unpredictable nature of humans, with all of their emotions, irrational thought processes, preconceived ideas and agendas. There are many theories and tools you can use to help you identify the best way forward, for example GOG's Ladder or Bruce Tuckman's Forming, Storming, Norming and Performing. These and others will help you understand how groups of people may behave as you move them along the path you want to or need to go.

Whichever process you follow, remember again there is no one size fits all process. You will have to try various different models and will likely end up with some kind of hybrid that works for you and your team. Don't become fixated on one method. As you are constantly working on improving yourself, work on bettering your team. Blending the right people into the right group for the right job is what makes a team great.

Asking the most appropriate questions will help you find and blend the right people into the group and will be the starting point of building a team.

Questions you should be asking include:

- What are the specific skills required for the job?

- What are the specific individual skills that the project requires?
  - o Will customer facing and non-customer facing skills be required in the same team, for example.

- Are there any people you already know who have those skills?

- Do those skills exist within the group of people you have inherited?

- Do the individuals in the group have team working skills?

- Is their attitude one that allows them to adapt to the team dynamic?

- How would they react in an emergency?

- Do they have a narrow understanding of the skills or are they broad thinkers?

- Are they problem solvers or problem creators?

- Do they have the ability to make decisions?

- Have they got the stick-ability to see the job through?

- What additional training do they require?

What attributes does an effective team leader need?

So we now understand what a team is and how to build a great team, but what are the attributes you as the leader need to develop in order to build a successful team and more importantly, to keep that team together?

The most important factor effecting any team is trust. It takes trust to build a team, to make a team remain a team and to make a team successful. You will need to trust yourself. That comes from working on improving yourself every day, being honest and open to advice and criticism. Developing trust in your team will also help you deal effectively with the conflicts, which will happen.

Leading your team effectively will also require coaching and mentoring skills as they grow and develop. Confidentiality, support and fair treatment are additional attributes which great team leaders exhibit.

Do you have to be perfect to develop a great team? No. Perfection is not a requirement of great team leadership.

CHAPTER 4

Leading Leaders – The Third Level of Leadership.

The third level, and often the most challenging level of leadership is leading other leaders.

Every leader will find themselves in a position where they will have leaders in their team or be promoted to a position where they are required to lead their peers. There is a massive difference between the skill of leading leaders and the skill of leading followers and you will be presented with an entirely different set of challenges.

The skills required for leading leaders are more fluid and intuitive than the skills for leading followers. Leaders are generally independent thinkers and are often more inquisitorial and have stronger opinions than followers. And although we find great examples of leaders who were skilled at leading other leaders throughout history, often resulting in great successes, there is no formula for leading leaders. We can take lessons and learn much from these historical figures, but must be careful not to become set in a methodology due to our admiration of them.

Leading leaders successfully requires finesse, thought and a deep desire to understand the leaders you are leading. Understanding their drivers, motivations, culture, ethics, communication style, etc, is critical to leading leaders successfully. And learning these skills and their application will determine the success or failure of your ability to lead other leaders.

For example, we can look again at 3 men from 3 different eras whom we briefly discussed earlier and who are universally recognised as great leaders of leaders. Abraham Lincoln, Winston Churchill and Nelson Mandela. Each of these men led followers and led other strong leaders successfully.

Abraham Lincoln was faced with a disintegrating nation and a potential civil war within months of taking office as the 16th President of the United States. How he responded to this crisis and the events which unfolded over the next few years, says much about his ability to lead not only followers, but leaders.

His predecessor, Buchanan, had faced a similar crisis at the begin of his presidency, particularly in the months after Lincoln's election, but prior to the inauguration, but did not have the strength of leadership to resolve these situations. In fact, he proved the fact that leadership has nothing to do with a position or a title. He was president in title, but could not be considered a leader and is believed by many to be one of the worst presidents in the nation's history [6]. He could hardly lead the ordinary people and had no hope of leading leaders.

Lincoln in turn is considered one of the greatest leaders and presidents of all time [6]. Six weeks after taking office and despite no previous military experience, Lincoln was called on to lead the nation in war and in politics successfully. His ability to balance these two huge challenges and leave a legacy on which his successors were able to build a united nation, is testimony to his leadership of followers and of leaders.

His skill lay in the ability to compromise when the situation required and to stand firm on those issues where compromise was not an option. In establishing his first cabinet, Lincoln reached out to all constituents of the party he represented and focused on unifying the differing opinions and political ideas. He even included all of his main rivals for his party's presidential nomination. All of the men he appointed were strong leaders with substantial followings both in society and politically, although some of these appointments turned out to be failures.

As mentioned earlier, Lincoln had no military experience and consequently had to do a large amount of 'on-the-job' training. He had to understand the movement of troops, supply line, communication strategies and battle tactics, all while the Southern armies were winning battle after battle against the armies of the North. This willingness to learn was accompanied by a willingness to acknowledge errors and accept blame. He was not the type of leader who deflected blame to others. Lincoln took responsibility.

These are crucial factors in leading leaders.

Winston Churchill, widely regarded as one of the most influential people in world history, too faced similar circumstances on being asked to form a government in May 1940 after a disastrous start to the 2nd World War for the British and Allied forces. He led the nation and most of the free world in its defiance of Nazi Germany and continued to face defeat after defeat as he re-organised his nation and its forces.

His advantage was his previous military, parliamentary and senior government ministerial experience. Churchill had served as a war correspondent during numerous campaigns around the world, as First Lord of the Admiralty during the early stages of the First World War, as a Lieutenant Colonel of the cavalry regiment on the

Western Front during 1916 and in the 1920's as Secretary of State for War and Secretary of State for Air. He was able to call on all of his experience to develop a clear understanding of what needed doing and of how to get it done, as well as understanding who he needed around him to ensure the job was completed well.

Churchill's experience in a coalition government during and after the First World War, now stood him in good stead as he forged his way through the coalition of the Second World War. A coalition cabinet filled with leaders, many of whom were opponents in the House of Commons coming from opposition parties. However, Churchill used his skill to lead these men, the country and much of the free world to victory in 1945.

During his career prior to the Second World War, Churchill had often lurched from failure to failure via the odd success story and it is these failures that gave him a unique perspective on dealing with defeat after defeat and of how to lead his leaders through those dark times. He learned the value and effect of words and became a master orator who swayed audiences and peers alike with his passionate speeches.

From his first speech in the House of Commons as Prime Minister on the 13 May 1940, in which he promised, '*I have **nothing to offer*** *but blood, toil, tears and sweat. We have before us an ordeal of the most grievous kind. We have before us many, many long months of struggle and of suffering.'* to the speech given in the House on the 4th June 1940, in which he skilfully described one of the greatest disasters in British military history, warned of possible invasion and remained steadfast in his belief of ultimate victory with these immortal words, *'We shall go on to the end. We shall fight in France, we shall fight on the seas and oceans, we shall fight with growing confidence and growing strength in the air, we shall defend our island, whatever the cost may be. We shall fight on the beaches, we shall fight on the landing grounds, we shall fight in the fields and in the streets, we shall fight in the hills; we shall never surrender,'* and again on the 20th August 1940, after victory in the Battle of Britain, he declared, *'Never in the field of human conflict was so much owed by so many to so few.'*

Never a man to shy away from the public eye, he learned how to skilfully use his visibility to encourage, inspire and build confidence in the nation and was often seen with other leaders either from his cabinet or from the military. So great was his impact, that his funeral saw the largest gathering of world statesmen in history.

And then there was Nelson Mandela in almost total contrast to

Lincoln and Churchill, yet again recognised as one of the greatest leaders in world history. Often described by the international media as the 'Father of the Nation,' Mandela endured 27 years in prison for what he believed in and dreamt of accomplishing, before becoming the first black president of South Africa in 1994.

Demonised by the government of the day as a vengeance seeking, communist inspired, terrorist, his legacy is one of compromise, forgiveness and reconciliation. He gained international acclaim not only for his activism against injustice and inequality, but also for his single minded focus on designing and building a country fit for all its people.

Unlike Lincoln and Churchill, Mandela never led his country or his people during a time of war, but lead them through some of the most challenging political and violent times, not just in the country's history but in world history, surrounding the 1994 election into a generally peaceful co-existence.

Mandela was a man who, like all great leaders, had the ability to look down the road and saw the future changes in world events, which would create a climate in which his dream could become a reality. He understood that the USSR, East Germany and the other Soviet Bloc countries which had materially supported the ANC would not last and their downfall would make South Africa less strategic to the West. These events, Mandela knew, would force the two parties to compromise and end Apartheid as well as the armed struggle.

This ability to anticipate these events allowed him to strategically position himself to take advantage when they happened. When offered the opportunity of early release with conditions by the then South Africa President P.W. Botha, Mandela declined the offer, understanding that neither the time nor the circumstances were appropriate. The depth of his leadership wisdom and anticipation are astonishing, as was the lack of understanding by P.W. Botha.

So what does this have to do with leading leaders, you are likely to be asking? Everything!

As Mandela exhibited wisdom, integrity and tenacity, many of the other leaders in his organisation, particularly those not in prison at the time, as well as the emerging younger white generation in South Africa, became convinced of his vision and the possibilities it could hold for all South Africans. They began, not only to see his vision, but believe it was a possibility.

Vision, wisdom and anticipation drew most of the leaders from business, political and social organisations in the country together and overcame their very obvious and significant difference.

For example, there was the gulf that existed between the ANC and the IFP (Inkatha Freedom Party). Not only did they distrust each other on political lines, but on tribal, cultural and historical lines as well. Everyday there were reports of one group attacking the other and the police had their hands full trying to keep the two groups apart. There was a virtual civil war between them and hundreds of people lost their lives in the process.

However, over a period of 2 - 3 years, the leaders of these organisations, Nelson Mandela and Mangosuthu Buthelezi, worked together to resolve their issues. It was primarily Mandela's vision, wisdom and integrity which won the day.

But perhaps the best example of the effects of his integrity and the trust leaders placed in his leadership, was exactly one year prior to the elections in 1994. On the 10th April 1993, anti-communist immigrant Janusz Walus, shot and killed ANC supporter and head of the South African Communist Party Chris Hani as he stepped out of his car in his driveway. With the country on the verge of tearing itself apart, riots in almost every city, town and village, cars burnt and shops looted, Mandela at great risk to his leadership of the ANC and to his credibility, addressed the entire nation via television, 3 days after the assassination.

"Tonight I am reaching out to every single South African, black and white, from the very depths of my being. A white man, full of prejudice and hate, came to our country and committed a deed so foul that our whole nation now teeters on the brink of disaster. A white woman, of Afrikaner origin, risked her life so that we may know, and bring to justice, this assassin. The cold-blooded murder of Chris Hani has sent shock waves throughout the country and the world. ... Now is the time for all South Africans to stand together against those who, from any quarter, wish to destroy what Chris Hani gave his life for – the freedom of all of us. ... This is a watershed moment for all of us. Our decisions and actions will determine whether we use our pain, our grief and our outrage to move forward to what is the only lasting solution for our country - an elected government of the people, by the people and for the people." (7)

And it was a watershed moment for both South Africa and Nelson Mandela. It revealed his dream was unwavering and that he was willing to lay it all on the line to make that dream a reality. As he spoke in this televised speech and one given earlier in the day, it became clear that it was no longer the President of South Africa, F.W. De Klerk, who was in control of the country. It was Mandela. Such was his stature and integrity, that most people including those who did not completely agree with him, followed. He had developed his authority to lead and lead he did.

An incredible leader, leading other leaders to see a vision realised.

We learn from Lincoln, Churchill and Mandela that great leaders lead other leaders by:

- Developing an authority to lead. This has nothing to do with a title, an education, a social status.

- Developing influence and persuasion.

- Effective communication which builds trust and establishes relationships.

Leaders will not follow you because of your position or charisma but because you develop in them an interest in where you are going. Leaders will follow you because they understand that it is in their interest to do so, not because you have been designated the leader or have said you are the leader.

CHAPTER 5

Leading
Organisations –
The Forth Level of
Leadership.

"Leadership is not magnetic personality. That can just as well be a glib tongue. It is not 'making friends and influencing people,' that is flattery. Leadership is lifting a person's vision to higher heights, the raising of a person's performance to a higher standard, the building of a personality beyond its normal limitations."

Peter F. Drucker

The first and most important discussion around leadership is how you lead yourself. As I said in the beginning of this book, all leadership begins with you as an individual. Your attitude, your actions and your results. When you get it right, your ability to lead a team and to lead other leaders is not just enhanced, but your leadership will draw followers and you will accomplish things beyond your wildest imaginations. And while these are vital skills to learn and develop and master in their own right, the pinnacle of leadership is leading an organisation which, in my view, makes it the second most important leadership discussion to have.

It is self-evident that if you have not learnt and effectively applied the skills of leading yourself, leading a team or of leading other leaders, it is highly unlikely that you would be able to lead an organisation of any size, in any field, very well. Leading an organisation is not in any way the same as managing an organisation. There is a clear line between these two skill sets and we should take care not to confuse them.

Most people can manage an organisation, even if it is done badly, but only people who have developed leadership skills can lead organisations. It is true that in order to lead an organisation, you would generally have a management function within the organisation, for example CEO, Chairperson or President, and I would suggest that most good organisational leaders are at the very least decently skilled managers, but management is not an essential criterion for the leadership of an organisation.

The fact is that drawing a comparison between leaders and managers has been done by many researchers, academics, authors and consultants and most who understand the different skill sets, have done a good job of presenting those differences fairly well. From Warren Bennis, author and widely regarded as a leader in the field of leadership studies, to Peter Drucker, who has been described as 'the founder of modern management' and Professor of leadership and author John Kotter, for example, are all well known for strongly advocating these differences and have illustrated their conclusions in a variety of different ways.

In studying leadership and management for over 25 years, including reading a wide and varied array of books, articles and lectures of the above mentioned experts as well as of authors, writers and experts with different views, I have found the following differences between the two concepts and have constructed this chart as an illustrative summary of my findings:

	Leadership	Management
Definition	Leadership is the individual skillful application of wisdom, influence and knowledge to foresee the possibilities and empower others to contribute in making the possibilities reality.	Management is the formal and positional process of skillfully moving a group of one or more people and/or entities using direction and control to achieve a specific goal.
Personality Type	Change and challenge	Stability and consistency
Orientation	People, vision, values	Task, objectives, protection

Focus	Leading empowered people, long-term success. The why, not the how to or what with	Organises systems, structure, process, workflow, short-term success. The how to and what with
Outcome	Direction and new roads	Results, old roads and the bottom line
Orientation to tasks	Challenges status quo, looks for new and better ways, empowers people through excitement, motivation and drive to solve problems. Lead between and toward change.	Creates processes, policies and methods to reduce risk and ensure solutions work. Copes with complexity. Manages within change.
Orientation to risk	Failure is the price of success, breaks the rules, reduces boundaries	Failure in not an option, makes the rules, creates boundaries
Orientation to people	Trust, respect, engage, generates enthusiasm, empowerment	Position, demand, manipulates or facilitates, directs
Decision making	Asks why and why not	Asks how and what with
Authority through	Intentional Influence, empowerment and personal charisma	Title, position and contract
Achievement	Accepts responsibility for failure, shares credit for success	Shifts blame for failure and accepts credit for success

Organisational perspective	Leaders have followers, leads and facilitates change, builds strategic relationships	Managers have subordinates, negotiates and manages change

It is clear from the list above and other lists like it, there are significant differences between the skills of leadership and those required for management, however, that does not mean that a leader should or could not have management skills and vis-versa. As mentioned previously, leading an organisation most often requires the leader to have some management skills. These different skills are applicable to differing circumstances and at different times and although this book focuses on leadership, leaders should never underestimate the value of good management skills or of their correct application. The fact is, that trying to run an organisation with either leadership or management is like trying to prune a rose bush with half a pair of secateurs. It makes no sense at all. Leaders need management and management need leadership. The two go hand in glove, but must be understood separately.

The challenge does not come, though, from knowing there are differences between leadership and management or what those differences are. The challenge is understanding when leadership is required and when management is required. Many people with great management skills apply those skills to scenarios in which leadership is required, often with major negative, and on occasions disastrous, consequences and again the alternative is equally true. Be careful never to confuse the two skill sets with each other.

Every organisational leader, should understand this fact and if, as a leader, you don't have the management skills needed, get someone in who does or work hard at developing those skills. Management skills compliment leadership skills. It does not replace them nor do leadership skills replace management skills.

So how do you lead an organisation?

Without wanting to repeat myself, but needing to do so for the purpose of answering the question. In order to effectively lead an organisation, you should have developed a significant level of self-leadership, which is under constant development and consequently will have developed a significant level of authority to lead, before being recognised as the leader of the organisation. This does not mean that you have led an organisation in the past. It simply means, that people recognise you as a leader, accept your leadership and follow you. Without the authority to lead, your role will be a management role.

And if you have been parachuted into an organisation for any number of reasons, you will need to work even harder to establish your credibility as a leader. Building relationships of trust with people in the organisation as soon as possible will be your friend and could expedite the process. Don't expect automatic acceptance!

As I mentioned in the previous chapter, leadership is not inherent in a title. Simply being appointed as CEO, MD, Director or manager in a business context or Minister, Secretary, MP, senator, etc, in a political context, will not make you a leader nor will having a professional title, for example lawyer, doctor or accountant. A title facilitates and allows you the authority to manage, instruct and direct people and organisations, but not to lead. Leadership is about the people who follow you because they want to, not because they have to. It's about how they follow you and whether you allow them to challenge you without becoming defensive or confrontational.

There are innumerable examples of organisations appointing an individual, who may have been a great manager of a department or division or even of another organisation, to the role of CEO or MD, only to find the person cannot lead, has no vision and does not inspire people to follow with often disastrous consequences. It is equally true, that many people who have great leadership skills and are recognised as leaders, have been elevated to management roles with similarly disastrous consequences. It's about the correct and effective application of the right skills at the appropriate time.

Have you ever heard it said, *'Jack/Jill has been promoted to a level above their competence?'* This often occurs when people with good skills as a manager or as a leader are elevated to the wrong role or not trained to understand the skills required for the role. It is generally not a matter of competence, but rather a matter of training, development and application.

Leading an organisation, therefore, requires that you not only have a vision of where you want the organisation to go in the next year or two, but that you also have a longer term view as far as 10 years into the future. You must understand the cultural, competency and resource requirements of the organisation and be willing to make the tough decisions necessary to ensure those are in place to support the best and most sustainable route forward. This includes surrounding yourself with the people competent for the job or task at hand. You need to understand the consequences of your vision and the decisions you make and how to delegate effectively. And you will need to accept the responsibility for those consequences, whether good or bad.

I mentioned culture in the previous paragraph and have often been asked about culture and cultural fit in an organisation or business. What it is, how it works and how it impacts on a leader? It is an appropriate discussion at this point as it will enhance your understanding of how leading an organisation works.

In defining an organisations culture or cultural fit, we must first put in place some foundations for this definition to rest on. Organisational culture has nothing nor should it have anything to do with racism, sexism or any other discriminatory tactic for hiring and firing nor should it be a term used to indicate a lack of diversity. However, defining cultural fit is a challenge as the concept has become extremely popular and so widely used in the past few years that it has become fuzzy enough around the edges so as to almost mean anything.

I recently read an article by author Ron Friedman PhD, titled '5 Myths of a Great Workplace' [8] in which he attempted to dispel 5 myths of the worksplace. Of particular relevance here was the 4th out of these 5 myths, 'They hire for cultural fit.' Friedman suggests that hiring for cultural fit is a myth as it could be counterproductive. 'There's a point at which too much similarity can stifle performance. For one, similarity fosters complacency,' the article says.

While in general I agree with the conclusion Friedman has drawn about similarity, I think he has missed the point about a cultural fit or the culture within an organisation. The article assumes that a cultural fit has to do with skills, qualification, experience, age, race or any other linear, tangible and identifiable construct. The fact is, cultural fit is not restricted to any one or even a collection of these. They do form a part of culture, but certainly do not define it.

Referring back to the beginning of the book, I mentioned that we as humans are non-linear, free thinking, sometimes predictable and often utterly unpredictable creatures. The same is true with culture and fit within an organisational context. It is an intangible concept which takes diverse people and somehow makes it 'feel' right. It takes a group of people who don't necessarily think alike, are dissimilar from each other, but may generally have broadly similar values and beliefs and somehow make it work. Here creativity and conflict, live contentedly side-by-side and do not tear individuals, the team or the organisation apart. Cultural fit or a lack thereof is the human interaction that holds organisations together or blows them apart. It is, like humans, unpredictable and intangible, but you know when it works.

A few years ago, I worked with a group of legal practices during a merger. The merging companies had differing cultures which, in some respects were at opposite ends of the scale, although in many respects were broadly similar. The obvious similarities were around their professional requirements and compliance, etc. These did not affect the culture of the businesses, but in other areas, their culture was affected.

For example, in one of the legacy practices partners, department heads and managers were referred to by their title and in another, each person was recognised by first name or by a nick name. As I, along with the directors of the new organisation, set about integrating these cultures, we very quickly identified a number of these issues and had to develop new policies which directly influenced the culture of the organisation. We also began to identify certain people who, although highly qualified and competent, just could not make the change to the new culture that began emerging.

It was not a tangible 'thing' we could immediately put our collective finger on. Some of these people had been with the legacy organisations for a number of years and it was not that they inexplicably developed bad relations with their colleagues. We just knew they would not fit and within a relatively short period all had left of their own accord.

I have also often heard CEO's, HR's managers and recruitment consultants, speak of the need to recruit for the culture of the organisation and while at a certain level this is true, good leaders and managers have to ensure they don't use it as a discriminatory tool. In an article written by Dan Lyons titled, *'When it comes to age bias, tech companies don't even bother to lie,'* [9] he recounts the experience he had when employed as a 52 years old at the tech company HubSpot. Dan reports an occasion where HubSpot CEO, Brian Halligan, in an interview with the New York Times regarding the age imbalance at the company, made it clear they were recruiting and retaining *'Gen X'ers'* for a cultural fit, because *'in the tech world grey hair & experience are overrated.'*

It is my view, and the view of the article author, that this is using culture as a discriminatory tool and nothing else. I have had a similar experience in coming to live and work in the UK and trying, initially to find a job. Age was always a factor in 'cultural fit' as was national identity. Cultural fit is more than a linear definition.

The bigger picture

The bigger picture is in essence a focus on the long term sustainability of the organisation, while appreciating the impact on the future of people, products and services in the here and now. It's knowing where you want to take the organisation, *that is having a vision for the future,* the route you intend taking to get there, *that is strategy* and the requirements needed to make the route and destination a reality, *that is the people, the products and services.*

And it is on these 3 pillars that success rests. Vision, strategy and the people, products and services. But for the leader, vision comes first. The rest are management skills.

I defined the concept of vision earlier in the book, so will not do that again, but will elaborate the idea of leadership vision more here as it is crucial for any leader to understand what vision is, but it is critical for organisational leaders to have a clearly defined and often communicated vision.

Vision is the most powerful tool available to a leader and is what drives innovation, invention, adaptation, progress and the strength to stand through tough times and to rise again after failure. It is a compelling vision which will make the world stand up, watch and take notice. Without it people cast off restraint, purpose and ambition for a better tomorrow. Without a compelling vision no-one goes anywhere, does anything and nothing of any sustainable value is accomplished.

Without a vision we would not have Apple or Microsoft, intercontinental flight, sewing machines, light bulbs, Rainbow Nations or motor vehicles. We would not have double glazing, electric cars, libraries, printed material, etc. All of those and so much more, were once the imagination of a person who saw the possibilities and who had the courage to make them a reality. Nelson Mandela saw the possibilities of an integrated nation, free for all races, John F Kennedy dreamed of putting a man on the moon, while Mother Teresa of giving comfort, food and clothing to the poor of India and Martin Luther King Jr dreamt of a time where men and women were judged by their character and not the colour of their skin. Bill Gates saw the possibilities of a computer in every home and on every desk while Steve Jobs' vision was *'to get a computer in the hands of everyday people.'*

For all of these leaders and for every leader not mentioned here, it all started with vision. It started with why. Vision is what gets leaders out of bed in the morning and it is vision that very often keeps them awake at night. And if you are to lead an organisation, you will need to have a vision of what you want to accomplish through that organisation or business. It is the organisational leaders vision that will drive productivity, creativity, innovation and ultimately success.

Now, it is possible to get all emotional, lofty and carried away about having a vision for the organisation, but it is the first and foremost skill of leadership. I say this because as a trainer and coach, I have heard business men and women share their vision of where they want to take a company and my immediate thought has been, 'you are floating away with the fairies!' It often sounds as if they are speaking words just to say they have a vision. No thought, no consideration, no inspiration! Just words.

A compelling vision is not a jumble of random ideas thrown together in the hope that something good will occur. It is not about chasing the unattainable and impossible. No matter how great my vision is to become a world heavy weight boxing champion is or how much I train, it is unattainable and impossible. I am too short, will never be in the right weight group, am to old and frankly don't like being punched repeatedly in the face or anywhere else for that matter. But this is what many people believe their vision should be like. Some kind of grandiose idea, which no matter how hard you work or how much money you throw at it will never become a reality.

A compelling vision has power and inspires, clarifies and draws people in to make it a reality. When Kennedy made his, *'I believe that this nation should commit itself to achieving the goal, before this decade is out, of landing a man on the Moon and returning him safely to Earth,'* speech in congress on the 25th May 1961, the hearts and minds of engineers and future astronauts were stirred at the possibilities. This vision drove men to develop systems, processes and programs which at the time did not exist or were in their infancy. This vision drove men to achieve what many believed to be impossible including bringing the crew of Apollo 13 home safely despite all the odds. You see, a compelling vision inspires passion and passion can change the world.

With this in mind, how would you know that the vision you have is one that can be realised and is the right vision for the company or organisation?

It is not an easy exercise and requires time and thought. Great leaders have given real thought to their values, ethics and beliefs and they align these with values of the organisation. When the vision they have fits into these, they ask question like, 'Will this stretch me and the organisation and provide the inspiration to challenge individuals to make it a reality?' 'Does this align with the company's current products and services?' And so on.

An organisations vision must also be realistic, which means the work and effort required to make it a reality, must be possible. When Kennedy made his vision clear, rocket technology had been used and the USSR had proven man could survive in space. Technological advances needed to be made, but it was possible. It is the reality of the potential within a compelling vision which followers recognise and grab hold of.

Once you have established your vision and have shared it with your management team, then you and they can begin to build the strategy and decide on the products and services which will make it a reality. This is where goals and plans make their entry into the process.

It is also here that the hardest part of a vision comes into play. Be prepared for negative reactions and questions. If you know what your vision is about and you are comfortable with it, communicate it with passion and deal with the questions and reactions with confidence.

Henry Ford was seriously criticised by friends and family as well as his shareholders and colleagues when he announced that he wanted to build a gas-powered automobile that everyone could afford and could be produced on a massive scale. So bad was some of the reaction to his vision, he left the company and had to start all over again. He knew his vision was possible, but would require another group of people to work and succeed with.

The assembly line, called flow line production back then, had been around since the 1850's and was in use in other environments, in particular meatpacking. Ransom E Olds had used the assembly line concept to build the Oldsmobile Curved Dash in 1901 and

Ford had already produced a variety of models prior to the mass produced Model-T. The Model N, for example, sold for as low as $250 in 1908 and over 7000 were produced or the Model B in 1904 which sold for the astronomical sum of $2000! He knew he could build them 'cheap or expensive' and he knew that mass production was possible. His challenge and the challenge of his management team was to effectively integrate these two into a seamless and profitable manner. Cheaply!

Ford and his team grabbed this idea, this vision by the throat and shook it until they found a way of making it work. Within a few short years they had developed the system so well that it took just 93 minutes [10] to assemble a complete car. His vision endured through the negative criticism because it was thoughtfully considered, passionately and persistently pursued.

You see, it is not the size or the cost of your vision that will ensure its success. It is your thoughtfulness in developing a clear and understandable vision and the passion and persistence to pursue it until it becomes a reality.

To be successful as the leader of an organisation, regardless of your title, focus on these 10 aspects:

- Self-leadership

- Your ethics and values

- Your vision and goals

- The organisations vision and goals

- Generating innovative ideas to achieve the vision

- Effective communication through all levels

- Consistently empowering others to become great by decentralising and delegating authority

- Anticipate success from everyone

- Draw leadership from others

- Persist until you succeed

CHAPTER 6

Developing New Leaders – The Fifth Level of Leadership.

"The single biggest way to impact an organisation is to focus on leadership development. There is almost no limit to the potential of an organisation that recruits good people, raises them up as leaders and continually develops them"

John C Maxwell

Most leaders and managers can make an organisation look good or profitable for a period of time, whether a few months or a few years. Launching new and invigorating products or programs, by process and system changes, cost cutting, by constantly losing the bottom 10% of performers every year, drawing in new clients with flashy promotions, etc, will all do the job. However, only one action will consistently make an organisation look good and be attractive to the best potential employees and investors. And that is the way in which the organisation and its leaders develop a pipeline of new leaders.

In other words, that the organisation and you at the top of the organisation in particular have a clear program of leadership development for those who meet the criteria. Products, programs, promotions and even people come and go, but the way in which you develop leaders will impact not just the organisation as a whole, but individuals and communities in specific. It is also your legacy which will live on after you have moved on from the organisation.

As we move further into the 21st Century, the focus of leadership and our understanding of what great leadership is has taken another shift. While it has always been an important component of all great leaders, developing others into leaders is taking on a far greater significance and the impact of the people who have been mentored into leadership is having a greater effect on the world around us, particularly as the X and Millennial generations enter the work and leadership space.

Developing others to become leaders is not about developing clones or about growing people who see the world our way and do everything the way we do it. It is about helping individuals to develop great skills, independent thoughts and innovative actions within a safe environment, where they are encouraged to be as good as they possibly can be. And yes, I understand this does sound idealistic, but this is the reality of what I see leadership demanding of itself in the decade ahead.

German philosopher and writer Johann Wolfgang Von Goethe once wrote, *'Treat people as if they were what they ought to be and you help them to become what they are capable of being.'*

This is the skill of leadership development! This is about the legacy of your involvement in a person's life and the impact you potentially could have. You will be remembered by and for the impact you had on the people around you and developing others into great leaders will ensure your influence lives on for years to come. In 5, 10 or 20 years' time, when you have moved on from the organisation, it is this that will remain.

With that in mind, here are a few questions, I believe every leader should be asking themselves daily:

- How well are my people learning from what I do?

- Are they learning from who I am becoming?'

- What are the lessons they are teaching others, which they have learned from me?

- Are they doing as I do or are they doing as I say?

- If I leave, what will be the abiding memory people have of me?

- How am I doing at leading myself?

- How am I doing as a leader?

- What can I learn today from others that will make me a better leader?

You see, you will be remembered momentarily for the numbers you produced, the profit or loss you left behind, but you will be remembered for a very long time for the lives you impacted and the influence you had. Very few people will remember your authority, but they will remember the lessons, both good and bad, they learned. Buildings deteriorate, systems become dated and lose their effectiveness and machinery generally has a limited life span, but the leaders you develop will be one of the few appreciating assets you can leave with an organisation.

As I have researched and considered many of the great leaders of the past 200 years, one overarching characteristic stood out above everything else. It stood out above their vision, their accolades, their awards and accomplishments. Without fail, every great leader I have looked at, had an almost laser like focus on adding value to the lives of the people around them and in doing so, developing other great leaders who would follow and become their legacy. In almost every leadership interview I have done and discussions I have had with leaders I have coached, trained or worked with, I have consistently found they have been impacted or mentored by a great leader or by a number of great leaders as they themselves have grown as leaders.

The fact is, that the best and most effective leaders are not content with self-development or even leading and developing teams or organisations. Their contentment is derived from seeing others develop into good and strong leaders through their commitment, mentorship and teaching. Your skill in developing other leaders will lay in your ability to mentor, coach and work with those around you who want to lead and become better leaders. As you grow in your leadership, the people who want to be mentored by you will appear and it is the great leaders who have their eyes open enough to see these opportunities as they are presented and have the courage and conviction to jump on them.

However, as a leader, it is easy to become complacent or distracted by the immediate and pressing issues which we all face in our various roles. You may also not realise that which is obvious to you because of your experience, knowledge and understanding, is not necessarily obvious to others with less experience and consequentially you may forget to teach and mentor.

It is also here that many leaders miss the opportunity to recognise future leaders and the opportunity to teach. The perception has long been held that a leader should by default see the obvious and be able to develop a solution, have an answer or provide direction in the situation. In life, business, relationships and in leadership, there are few things which are immediately obvious outside of experience, knowledge and understanding of the particular environment. Our ability to see the 'obvious' grows with our contextual experience and knowledge and if we as leaders disregard individuals as a consequence of them not seeing these 'obviouses', we risk missing potentially great leaders.

Viewed from a military perspective. New privates do not command armies, regiments, companies or even small 3 and 4 man teams. They grow over time by observing the leaders around them and attending specific courses designed to give them knowledge in an area of their profession. They take that knowledge and in a safe environment, learn to exercise it practically. When they are deemed competent, they may get promoted and lead a small team or platoon. Over time, they grow into becoming the leader who sees the obvious (on most occasions) due to their experience and application of knowledge.

In a surgical context, newly qualified medical students don't perform surgery on patients until they have spent time with senior surgeons, who have the responsibility of training and coaching them through procedures. The students observe and show their growing knowledge through answering ever increasingly difficult questions. Only when they have begun to prove their competence are they allowed to begin performing minor surgery, until the basics of diagnosis and remedy become obvious. Personally, I prefer it that way!

Why then is it that we, in an organisational capacity think it works differently?

The dictionary describes a legacy as *'anything handed down from the past, as from an ancestor or a predecessor'* [4]. As you grow in your leadership skill and ability, so your legacy can begin to grow. It is when that experience and skill is handed down to those around you and you develop them into leaders, that your legacy is cemented. Many people think of a legacy as something which is gained only on the death of a person, however, in leadership a legacy is developed and left during your leadership lifespan.

As I have repeatedly mentioned, leadership begins with you

continually re-engineering yourself to be better than you previously were. In the same way, your legacy is shaped not by the end result, but by the road you and those around you travel. The decisions and mistakes you make and the challenges you overcome are all part of the legacy you develop. Abraham Lincoln, Winston Churchill and Nelson Mandela's leadership legacy lives on long after they have gone and continues to influence millions of people around the world.

The story of former PepsiCo CEO and chairman, Roger Enrico, and the Disney Institute are two of the best examples of developing a pipeline of new leaders within an organisation.

In both case, the central idea and theme behind developing a pipeline of leaders is; *'the most important skill and responsibility of a leader is to personally model and communicate behaviours and values of the organisation in such a way as to develop other leaders.'* This way of looking at leadership development has and still is challenging those in leadership roles to re-evaluate conventional wisdom and think seriously about how to move their organisations forward more effectively.

These organisations have recognised the importance of the leaders at the top of the organisation investing a large percentage of their time personally conducting workshops, training sessions and coaching future leaders inside the organisation. It is said that in the late 1990's, Roger Enrico invested as much as 100 days a year, training and coaching senior executives and other leaders throughout the organisation [11].

The question I challenge all leaders with is, how much of your personal time do you invest in developing your leadership pipeline? All too often the answer I get goes something like, 'My HR department deals with that,' or 'I use XYZ company for our training requirements.' I seriously question whether the 'leaders' who respond in that way are actually leaders or whether they are managers filling a leadership role!

Like Enrico and Disney, the best leaders understand that leadership development within their organisations is not about spending time, but rather investing time which will generate far greater returns in the future than the time spent doing other 'things' or sending leaders on external leadership training courses. As a trainer, I am all for external training programs as the trainer will often see issues, challenges and skills internal people would not, due to preconceived ideas, personal knowledge, etc. The fact though is, the best training is done by the leaders within the organisation who understand the values, culture, ethics, vision and mission of the business. This is very difficult for an external trainer to communicate. It is of course conditional on the leader personally growing and developing themselves.

So how do you, as a leader develop a pipeline of great leaders no matter how large or small your business, organisation or team is?

You could think of it as similar to teaching an adult to ride a bicycle for the first time in their life. Recently, in a park near to where we live, I watched a mother trying to teach her young daughter to ride a bike. The bike had training wheels, was the right size for the daughter and the mother had her own bike, so knew how to ride. Should have been easy, right? I watched for about 30 minutes before the mother gave up and the child was in tears. She tried everything she could think of, to no avail.

The more experience you have in riding a bike, theoretically, the easier it should be for you to teach. However, there is a huge gulf between doing and teaching or educating in almost every area of life, including teaching someone to ride and sadly, most people are not willing to learn how to teach. It is not only about teaching them to balance, but to steer, peddle, brake and be aware of their surroundings, amongst other things, all while trying not to fall and hurt themselves.

You also have to encourage them and deal with the inherent fear of the potential to fall and injure themselves. Obviously the younger the person you are teaching, generally the easier it is to gain the skill of riding, so start learning to teach, as soon as you can. The temptation for you, may also be to get on the bike and try to show them how. And while this will work to show the basics, you have to let them get in the driving seat and make the hard mistakes.

I few days after watching the lady and her daughter in the park, I saw them again, and this time was different. The little girl had a few plasters on her knees and elbows, but was peddling confidently, if wobbly, along the tar pathway. She had learned and the pride on her mother's face was something to behold. The mother had learned how to teach her in a way she understood and off she went.

The fact is, if they are allowed to persistently keep trying and learning with ever decreasing physical support and encouragement from you, they will eventually get it and be off on their own before you know it.

In the same way, as a leader, teaching or educating people to become leaders is a skill you should work hard at learning. You need to know how to show, how to delegate, how to guide and eventually how to let go.

It is important to remember that as with the definition of leadership there are a multitude of differing ideas around how and when to develop new leaders within an organisation. This is primarily due to almost every organisation having different priorities, values and objectives which will impact on their specific leadership requirements. There, however, are some broad basics which are applicable across all environments.

These 6 questions form the framework of The Audacious Leadership Development program and are the 'how to' of leaders developing new leaders within an organisation.

1. Are you personally teachable?

This is the most difficult part of developing other leaders. You will have to learn new skills in communication, grow in your theoretical knowledge of leadership, understanding all aspects of the organisation and be prepared to be challenged, amongst other things.

Most people, including many leaders, believe the illusion they are great communicators, which should therefore make training very easy. The facts are so far removed from the illusion. The truth is that most people don't understand the art of communication and as a result, speak at people instead of speaking with them. Training is not just about you telling people what you think they should know and do, but more importantly listening and understanding what they already know or don't know, what thoughts and ideas they have, what their values and priorities are, etc. This is the art of communication and talking with, rather than at or to people.

Learn better communication skills and you will revolutionise your teaching skills.

You will not only need to understand the aspects of leadership with which you agree, but also those with which you don't agree, as not everyone will see it your way and if they don't, you need to be well prepared to argue your case and understand theirs.

However, the main reason you want to be teachable is, it sets the right example and shows that as a leader you will never 'arrive' and need to continually grow and develop as an individual.

2. Are you willing to invest the time, effort, energy and emotion it takes to successfully develop new leaders?

Most people in leadership roles, as we saw earlier, have the belief it is a training or HR departments job to take care of leadership development or that it is an expense they begrudgingly pay an external provider to supply. It is often seen as a cost for which they see very little immediate return. I have often found the attitude to leadership develop is, it costs too much to train people who leave after they have used us to gain experience or as I was told in one case, 'Leadership development does not work. I know because it did not work for me!'

No, I am not kidding. The CEO of a multi-national who funded as little as he could reasonably get away with, who had an executive MBA in Strategic Leadership and numerous other degrees, did not believe in leadership training because it had not worked for him. All that money and effort and he had gained nothing! Unbelievable right? Not really as it was not the first time I had heard something like that.

And within these reasons mentioned above lays the single reason most leadership development training programs fail. People often learn very little or what they do learn is not relevant to their particular environment.

It is good to send individuals on training courses and for them to interact with other growing leaders from different environments and for internal training to be provided, but you as a leader have to be intimately involved and invested in the program and the process. It will mean time, effort, energy and emotional commitment, but if you are fully committed to it, the rewards are enormous. You should understand what they have learned and help them find ways of applying the principles in your environment. That will ensure the value of the training they have received.

If you are fully invested in this process, you will be properly prepared for the time you have with the people you are teaching, mentoring and coaching. You will keep a journal of their progress and will monitor their improvement. You will know when to demonstrate, when and how to delegate and when to let them do things on their own.

There will be disappointments and you will feel the emotional impact of those times, but there will be times of great success and you will need to help them manage the emotional and psychological impact of those times.

3. Are you willing to be a vulnerable role model, coach and mentor?

Vulnerability is a key strength of a great leader. It means that, while you don't bleed all over people, you are emotionally and psychologically strong enough to accept your mistakes, weaknesses and short-comings, even when they have a negative impact.

It also means you are willing to accept and acknowledge that you don't know it all and you don't have all the answers. It is not about being 'weak' as a leader, but rather about being strong. It takes great courage and self-control. It makes you real and destroys the demi-god status many people in leadership roles try to cultivate.

It is about owning who you are and it will make you a great role model as people watch you work through and overcome your weaknesses and challenges. It will give you the right to coach and mentor. It is scary, but it is worth it.

4. Do you have the capacity to create and develop a training program from which those you are developing can learn in a clear and structured way?

If not, are you willing to learn? You don't need to draft an entire word for word training manual, but you will need to be able to develop a fairly structured program and understand the outcomes you want to see. Bring in the people that can help you in this process if you need to, but it must be a program which meets your requirements and the outcomes which will best benefit the organisation.

I have often seen leadership development programs fail or prove ineffective as a result of not being designed with the outcomes which best benefit the individual or organisation in mind. Many of these courses, while consisting of great and valuable material, are off-the-shelf programs, which are generic and don't allow for any kind of depth of learning particular to your organisation.

If you are involved in the design and the delivery, albeit not all of the delivery, the value of the content and the experience, will escalate exponentially.

The question though is, 'Are you willing to do what it takes?'

5. Do you understand both soft and hard leadership skills?

This is a question which develops out of the previous point. Many leadership development programs are designed to focus on the 'hard' skills needed as a leader and to relegate the 'soft' skills to an inferior role. The problem is with the words, 'hard' and 'soft' and not with the skills themselves. These words give the impression of one being superior to the other. The fact is, that great leaders understand that both hard and soft skills are needed in their leading and impact on their leadership as well as on how they teach and coach new leaders.

There is nothing inferior or superior about these differing skills in any way. The hard skills are often defined as the occupational type skills, that is the skills which get the job done, while the soft skills can be defined as the emotional or behavioural type skills, for example, dealing with relationships.

Making decisions would be an example of a hard skill. Taking responsibility for the consequences, whether good or bad, for those decisions, is another example of soft skills at work. For example, you should develop the hard skill of having the tough conversations while developing the soft of showing empathy and honesty during that conversation.

The 2 are equally important and are inclusive of each other.

6. Can you raise your game to inspire and enthuse others?

This question picks up from point 3 above. Enthusiasm and inspiration, like humour, do not come naturally to everyone, but should be integral to your leadership.

There is no need to climb Mount Everest, represent your country in sport, cycle the breadth of the country or any other great achievement to be an inspiration to the leaders you are teaching or mentoring, but you will need to inspire in them the confidence to become great leaders. By becoming a great leader, yourself.

If you lead with enthusiasm they will pick up on it and will become enthused. I am not talking about walking around with a pasted on smile. I am talking about real, honest enthusiasm for the company, the products, the people and the clients. It becomes infectious.

Great leaders develop others by:

o Planning the individual's development with them.

o Investing time in those individuals.

o Focusing on enhancing the individuals existing skills, before developing new skills.

o Developing a culture of development by rotating people through different positions and roles. Challenge their ability to learn and grow. Challenge them to do those jobs which others won't do or are unfamiliar with.

o Encouraging them to make decisions and to take bold action in a way that comes naturally to them. Then giving great feedback that is positive and encouraging.

o Having tough conversations when they are required.

Audacious Delegation

Finally, a word or two on delegation. While I am aware that this topic could fit in earlier, I do feel it is most appropriate here. This is not a comprehensive look into delegation, but is rather designed to give an overview of what delegation is and how it works.

A large part of your job in developing new leaders is to learn the skill of delegating. Great leaders understand delegation is an art that has great impact on the development of everyone, but particularly on the development of other leaders. They also understand the opportunities which effective delegation provides to individuals, teams and organisations.

The way in which managers and leaders delegate should be broadly similar, but is often in practice very different. Management style of delegation often implies a, *"Do this and do that and do as I say"* attitude which is not the right way in which to delegate, while leadership delegation skills should be focused on the growth of the individual being delegated too. Great leaders often deliberately surround themselves with people who are better than themselves in areas they are not particularly good at or are not interested in and grow these people through effective delegation.

Having said that, I have consistently seen that delegation is one of the largest stumbling blocks to leadership development and to organisational success in many organisations, as most leaders have not developed very good delegation skills or totally misunderstand the art of delegation. During many of my client interactions and interviews with leaders and senior executives, I have asked for their opinions on delegation and have discovered the following:

- Approx. 65% of SME business owners believe the age old adage, *'If you want something done properly, then do it yourself,'* and as a result only delegate a small percentage of the work requirements.

- Approx. 67% of directors feel the need to constantly check up on the people they have delegated work to as they are not confident it will be done correctly.

- Over 75% of entrepreneur's struggled to grow their businesses significantly due to a lack of trust.

With this in mind, let me briefly share with you the 5 levels of Audacious Delegation.

The 5 Levels of Audacious Delegation™

Andrew Carnegie once said, *"The secret of success is not in doing your own work but in recognizing the right man to do it."*

I have discovered there are 5 levels to delegation. When delegating any task, great leaders follow through these stages:

Level 1: Developing Confidence

This is the first level of leadership delegation. At this level you are beginning the process of gauging the leadership values of the people you are working with and are wanting to develop. There is little to no consequence in delegating as all the important 'stuff' has already been completed by you or someone you trust. In reality it is, *"Do exactly as I have asked you to do. Nothing else."*

You should, however, be looking for those people who, despite your instructions, will ask intelligent questions to test the task and the results. You should not be looking for them to challenge the process, task or results, but to ask questions that may bring more clarity. You may also find the opportunity to help them ask better questions and in so doing, create a learning experience for them.

This process will help you develop confidence in the person's ability to move to the next level of delegation. This is also, unfortunately the level at which most delegation not only starts, but stops. There is often a high level of expectation placed on people, by leaders who have little or no understanding of the different levels of delegation. By expecting people to perform without understanding their capabilities or without them understanding how you delegate, your expectations will not be met and the person to whom you are looking to delegate to will have their confidence set back.

Level 2: Discovery

The second level of delegation is the discovery level. At this level, you should discuss the task with the person to whom you are delegating, ask them to do all the necessary research and to report back to you. They will not yet be required to make any recommendations in their reporting back, however, there are no restrictions placed on them actually making suggestions.

This again provides the opportunity for you to gauge their leadership skills and an opportunity for you to create another learning experience. You are beginning to build a picture of the person and their leadership development as well as their drive. You are beginning to discover whether they are thoughtful, resourceful and creative.

Level 3: Creative Progress

At level 3, you have begun to place more responsibility on the individual. You would want them to research that task, form an opinion and make recommendations. You are looking for their innovative and creative thinking to make the task a success. From this level upwards, the consequences and importance of the tasks are increasing and you should expect regular, planned feedback on the progress of the research and the potential solutions.

You will require this feedback due to the growing importance of the task and will be challenging their thought processes along the way. This feedback allows you to step into the process at any stage if you see the process not working out or is veering off track.

It is also at this stage, where you should expect the individual, if appropriate, to begin delegating simple tasks at level 1 to others around them. This will help the person to begin their own program of developing new leaders downstream.

Level 4: Delivered Results

At level 4, you have developed the confidence in the person to such a degree that they now have the responsibility for doing the research, making the decisions and being accountable for the results. Without great detail, you would want feedback of the progress on an ad hoc basis and on completion. The tasks or projects they are delegated now range from significant to mission critical and will have a higher level of complexity. Their critical, strategic and creative thinking will now be visible and their strength of character will be tested.

They will, where appropriate, have developed a team whom they are now developing through levels 1 -3 all of which will be a part of them growing as a leader.

Level 5: Total Ownership

At this level, you have total confidence and trust in the person, not only to run with a task you have given them, but to initiate tasks and projects on their own as they see the needs developing. As a consequence of your trust and confidence in them, you do not require feedback except to be told when the task is completed. You should convey to the individual and their team your total support and confidence in them.

At this stage they will own not only the task or project, but the consequence of success or failure. They will know that should they need, you are available to listen and advise, but not to make their decisions nor to interfere.

There are 4 key components that form the basis at every level of Audacious Delegation. Without these basics, delegation would be less effective than it could be:

1. Communication.

2. Responsibility.

3. Authority

4. Accountability

CONCLUSION

I began this book with the story of 4 young, white soldiers caught up in a political conflict and who were rescued by a young black man who stood up to the crowd wanting to attack these soldiers. That was 1984. A world away from today and the mists of time could be said to have clouded the view and changed the perspective of what occurred that humid, dark and utterly terrifying night.

In 2006, I was in Johannesburg for a business meeting with a client whom I had met on a few occasions previously. As I sat on the terrace of a coffee shop waiting for my client, who had messaged me to let me know he was running very late for our appointment, an African gentleman walked toward me whom I instantly recognised. My mind went back to that night in 1984 and I knew I was about to meet the man who had rescued me and my 3 colleagues.

'You were one of the soldiers,' he said. 'You look bigger and older, but I know you.' He too recognised me. It was an incredible moment.

He sat down with me and over an hour, we spoke of that night and of the years that followed. Having no previous idea who he was, I discovered Andile* was the oldest son of a respected Xhosa chief who had great influence in the townships around Port Elizabeth and the Eastern Cape at the time. That evening he had been asked by his father to use his influence as a community leader to restore calm in the area.

As we spoke, I became aware not only of the physical courage it took Andile to walk into an environment where violence had descended, but to do so while confronting the crowd and persuading them not to act on their desires. I discovered that in the days which followed, Andile's life was threatened regularly, to the point where he had to go into exile. He remained out of the country and away from his family until 2001 when he returned and settled in the Johannesburg area.

Before we parted, I asked Andile why he had done this extra-ordinary thing. His response astounded me and I still think back on his words. *'I believed in a better tomorrow than we had on that day and I knew that tomorrow would never come unless we stood up and led people to that place. Killing was never the answer. Now we have a better tomorrow.'*

Andile's life was turned upside down by the choice he made that night in 1984. The choice to stand up for what he believed in and the dream that lived in his heart. The leadership skills he showed on that night and during the time relating to the fallout of his intervention, have remained with me ever since. Sadly, I never heard from him again, but know that at that time he still lived daily with that passion in his heart for a better tomorrow, despite the constant and persistent threat of danger to his life.

To find out more about me or to access

my videos, podcasts, audio series, free downloads

and courses, please visit my website www.vicwilliams.net

Also connect with me on LinkedIn
www.linkedin.com/in/vicwilliams1

or

follow me on Twitter https://twitter.com/AudaciousCo

REFERENCES

1. http://www.mckinsey.com/insights/leading_in_the_21st_century/why_leadership-development_programs_fail

2. http://www.biomedcentral.com/1471-2202/13/52

3. Proverbs 23:7 (NKJV)

4. http://dictionary.reference.com/browse/legacy?s=t

5. 'FIELD MARSHAL WILLIAM SLIM AND THE POWER OF LEADERSHIP' FREDERICK A. BAILLERGEON, LTC (Retired), USA page 5

6. https://web.archive.org/web/20100706090046/http:/www.siena.edu/pages/179.asp?item=2566

7. http://www.anc.org.za/show.php?id=4083

8. https://hbr.org/2015/03/5-myths-of-great-workplaces/

9. https://www.linkedin.com/pulse/when-comes-age-bias-tech-companies-dont-even-bother-lie-dan-lyons

10. https://books.google.co.uk/books?id=HQdTa9ZXIVAC&pg=PA29&redir_esc=y&hl=en#v=onepage&q&f=false

11. https://www.questia.com/magazine/1G1-18441765/the-pepsi-challenge-building-a-leader-driven-organization

Any name marked with an asterisk * has been changed to protect the identity of the individuals concerned. I accept that some readers may not understand, but there are personal and safety reasons for protecting some people's identity and I thanks you in advance for respecting that right to privacy.